"I shall not want"

"I shall not want"

In times of great need we turn to God for help. This collection of articles tells how Christian Science enables you to exchange lack and limitation for a life of unlimited good.

Divine Love always has met and always will meet every human need. MARY BAKER EDDY

The Bookmark
Santa Clarita, California

Copyright © 2002 by Ann Beals

All rights reserved under the International
and Pan-American Copyright Convention

Library of Congress Control Number: 20001119634

"I shall not want."
   p. cm.
   "In times of great need we turn to God for help. This collection of articles tells how Christian science enables us to exchange lack and limitation for a life of unlimited good."
   "'Divine love always has met and always will meet every human need'--Mary Baker Eddy."
   ISBN 0-930227-39-5

1. Christian Science. 2. Prayer.

BX6943.184 2002   289.5
                                  QB133-222

Published by
The Bookmark
Post Office Box 801143
Santa Clarita, California 91380

CONTENTS

Articles and Statements by Mary Baker Eddy
Article on Supply ... 1
Talk on Supply ... 3
Possession ... 4
Statements on Supply ... 5

Possession ... 9
by Adam H. Dickey

The Law of Supply and Demand ... 15
by Lucis C. Coulson

Sufficiency ... 17
by Julia M. Johnston

Supply as Spiritual Idea ... 20
by L. Ivimy Gwalter

The Divine Affluence ... 23
by Maria Soubier

The Science of Supply ... 26
by Martha Wilcox

Understanding Supply ... 29
Attributed to Martha Wilcox

Supply ... 36
by Ann Beals

PSALM 23

The Lord is my shepherd; I shall not want.

He maketh me to lie down in green pastures: he leadeth me beside the still waters.

He restoreth my soul: he leadeth me in the paths of righteousness for his name's sake.

Yea, though I walk through the valley of the shadow of death, I will fear no evil: for thou art with me; thy rod and thy staff they comfort me.

Thou preparest a table before me in the presence of mine enemies; thou anointest my head with oil; my cup runneth over.

Surely goodness and mercy shall follow me all the days of my life: and I will dwell in the house of the Lord forever.

FOREWORD

Healing in Christian Science is not confined to physical and mental illness. This Science helps us to overcome a chronic state of lack and limited means.

Mary Baker Eddy once wrote, "Our Father is rich and will not deprive us of one good thing, but will add continually to our storehouse of blessings. Everything belongs to God. It is ours now as His reflection for <u>there are no debts in divine Love</u>."

Financial struggle is not a normal way of life. When the study of Christian Science is brought to bear on this limited state of mind, the spiritual ideas that unfold can bring to us an ever-expanding sense of supply leading to a life of abundance.

This collection of articles is focused on helping you realize a more abundant life. The authors, writing out of their own experience in overcoming lack, provide the ideas and spiritual insight that enable you to do the same. This collection includes some of the most helpful articles on supply found in Christian Science.

ARTICLE ON SUPPLY

From *Essays on Christian Science Attributed to Mary Baker Eddy*

God is a business God. He attends to the business of the universe, and you reflect His business ability. The divine and perfect law of attraction is operating in and through the law of adjustment, bringing to me all that belongs to me. Today divine Mind adjusts me to my work, and adjusts my work to me. Under this law of adjustment, God's law, my work must be successful. Through steadfast declaration, work and worker are brought together. Thus supply meets demand and God's perfect law is brought into manifestation.

Our Father is rich and will not deprive us of one good thing, but will add continually to our storehouse of blessings. Everything belongs to God. It is ours now as His reflection for there are no debts in divine Love. Whenever there seems to be a lack or need in your experience, that simply indicates the scientific fact that the seeming need is already supplied by Love's gracious abundance. Then give thanks with your whole heart because you have learned in Christian Science that God's supply is ever at hand.

Evil argument and mental suggestion cannot frighten, swerve, deter or keep me from doing the work that is mine to do today. Divine Love, Mind, flows through every obstacle. I have nothing but Love to meet and nothing but Love to meet it with. My income is Life, Truth and Love. It is equal to any demand that can be made upon it. This income is my inalienable possession, derived from no earthly source, supplied through no material channel, dependent upon no human personality nor personal effort — not even my own — coming to me direct from God, neither to be hindered, stopped or turned aside; mine to receive, to possess, to use, to share, but never to hoard nor waste. It is to be received without doubt, possessed without fear, used without scruple, shared without apprehension that the supply can fail.

All things that the Father has are mine. These come to me and constitute my income. Unfailing, abundant, equal to all demands that can be made upon it. God gives wealth, *not money*, for He gives nothing that can fade or fail. Then since money seems to be a necessary commodity, how am I to regard it? It is a sign of value. Money is not value, it is a sign of value. Material possessions are not wealth but a sign of it. Then the possession of money means that I have access to the wealth of God, and that my Father which seeth in secret rewardeth me openly. He has given me the manifestation here and now that I have access to the hidden treasure — a secret bounty of divine Love.

Jesus did what he saw was best for his own spiritual welfare, no matter if the multitude did throng him. He left them and went up into the mountain to refresh himself. He did not look around and say, "Just see how many need help — no mount for me today or tonight." He left them and went and returned refreshed and helped them more.

It is necessary that you keep your eye single to the light and your whole body will be full of light. Don't look at self, look at Soul. Be not self-willed, be individually thinking your thoughts straight from God and not from mortals. It is just as erroneous to be governed by other people's wills as to be self-willed, for there is only one common foe, our self-will, not a human will in you and one in another, but our common self-will as opposed to the spiritual will which is the persistent keeping of the eye single to the light. Hold on to your Life. Let nothing rob you! Rise, not by will-power, but rise in exaltation. God loves you. He will not let you fall. The heart is a symbol of Love and to heal the weak heart we heal the weak sense of Life and Love. God loves you and you love Him. You are right in the heart of divine Love. You throb with active Love, the animating Principle. Life was never disturbed, never in pain, but pulsates in eternal harmony. These fearing times are only chemicalizations, like a big storm which gathers and breaks only to leave the atmosphere clear.

Now, worry does not demonstrate. All the mental energy one expends on worry would be better used in faith. Just pray when you do not know what to think, or sing a hymn to yourself until worry goes.

Nothing happens out of order, everything happens in the order of development for you. You pray to learn; then why be regretful when the page turns over and a hard lesson comes next? Let resentment go, and just roll up your sleeves, so to speak, and get to work and declare that you are going to squeeze all the benefit out of that experience that you can. Just learn to be glad of these chances to impersonalize error.

Do you spend much time on condemning yourself? That is self-murder. Our whole salvation lies in seeing ourselves as God made us, in His likeness, spiritual. If you find yourself beginning to grieve over yourself, refuse to look at it as you would a cut finger you want to heal. The doubts and fears you speak of are doubtless not your thoughts, but mental suggestions of other minds, whispered into your thought. To all such whisperings answer, "I don't believe you, you are a liar." "Greater is he that is in you than he that is in the world." Only Love can lift you above it all. Love, love, love. Let nothing crush you, *rise immediately*. Love has no poison to impart. The only Mind is Love, and Life, and purity.

TALK ON SUPPLY

From *Essays on Christian Science Attributed to Mary Baker Eddy*

I feel that, while you are not after money in the ordinary sense of the word, there is every reason to know that you are entitled to adequate provision. Everything that is involved in that which people call supply, maintenance, etc., is a thing of thought. What we need to do, is reach out toward unlimited thought, in this respect. Humanly, it would be natural for you to think that, while you are in the practice of Christian Science, your supply should come through your practice; but just see what a limited thought is that! Inasmuch as supply belongs to infinity, and is really a manifestation of infinity, how woefully scant is the thought that ignores infinity and limits supply to one narrow channel.

On the other hand, think thus: Supply is omnipresent and unlimited, and is always where you are and what you want. It is liable to show itself to you through millions of channels. Therefore, open up all the channels and let it come in. Keep yourself in a state of non-surprise. Gain a mental attitude in which nothing in the way of supply will surprise you, not even if you found pieces of silver in the mouth of a fish. You are not the victim of any circumstance; you are the child of God. You have an infinite income commensurate with the grandeur of your thought expressing the infinity of being. No sense of man or woman, or any belief of occasion, event, or inexplicable fatality, or any other belief, can hold out against your treatment, which is the very presence and power of the only God there is.

Infinity is wholly accomplished. Life is established, and all law and power are established. Reality, or the divine Mind, includes nothing but perfection. All the possibilities of being are yours now; there will never be any more. You need not wait for deliverance; today it is yours. You may as well express dominion now as to wait. Declare everything good for yourself. Expect everything good now.

POSSESSION

From *Essays on Christian Science Attributed to Mary Baker Eddy*

I believe that taking possession of what God gives us is the step to God giving us what we deserve. That is, if you take possession of what is at hand for you, it becomes the loaf and the fish to you — the basis of multiplication. Jesus' first question to the disciples in Matthew 15:34, was "How many loaves have you?" You must have the consciousness of possession of something to multiply.

Keep practicing, "This is mine," until the spirit of possession is gained, and you feel "All things are mine."

You will notice that Jesus gave thanks before he multiplied the loaves and the fishes, although the disciples had belittled the amount, saying it was not enough.

Taking possession, does not mean contending outwardly with another's right, but a settled consciousness of possession of your own things, your privacy, your time, your work, etc., that will make itself felt and hold its own against robbery. Call it injustice, robbery, or what you will that has pursued you, but the lack of the sense of possession *in you* has made all these things possible. *Man was made to have dominion.* How can he have dominion over what he does not possess? "All things that are mine are yours" (meaning, "All that I have is thine") means *just what it says.* Now

"I shall not want"

this does not mean a human sense of greed, but a consciousness of Mind that gives power and control.

It is wonderful how I have wakened up and forged ahead in every line since I took possession of this idea. I feel so much better physically and I am holding you in all things that are the Father's. Why should we not take possession of healing, of health, of demonstration, of results? Take possession of your life, don't let it stop because of disappointment; take it right up out of depression and darkness, and put it in the Light and govern it with Paul saying, "None of these things move me."

Take possession of results. The sense of loss is a lie. Let the result be what you decide and not another mortal's. Your land of Canaan lies before you — go in and possess the land.

STATEMENTS ON SUPPLY

Attributed to Mary Baker Eddy
From *Divinity Course and General Collectanea*

God is our source of supply, and supplies every need. He is infinite, and in Him there is no lack, no loss, no want. Mind holds all in position.

God is our Father and He is rich; His resources are inexhaustible, and whatsoever we ask for we shall receive. The devil tries to make us indifferent and ungrateful.

Your Father is rich and will not deprive you of one good thing, but will add continually to your storehouse of blessings; everything belongs to God, then it is yours now as His reflection, for there is no debt in divine Love.

Mrs. Eddy's Remarks on Supply

There is nothing within me that corresponds with, or responds to, any form of evil. There is no illusion of poverty. God made all, owns all there is, and it is good. I am joint-heir with Christ, in God, and have my share of everything. I am exempt from want, loss, lack or limitation of any kind. There is no material resistance that can limit me. 'The Lord is my Shepherd, I shall not want.' Abundance cannot lapse into lack, since God is my fountain source of infinite riches and plenty. I can and do demonstrate the wealth which comes from God with no interruption in its flow. I am prosperous and successful, kept so by an inexhaustible supply. There is no mental self-mesmerism. I have fullness of supply and abundance. There are no adverse circumstances, no avarice, no greed, no trust in money, nor love of money. I live in the land of promise.

God gives abundance of intelligence and opportunity. I cannot be impoverished mentally, physically, spiritually, or financially. God is substance and I reflect that substance.

Realize to yourself daily more than once that the fields are white and ready for the harvest, that divine Love always has met every human need, the need for work as well as any other; that Mind is ever active and you reflect divine activity; that the source of supply supplies every need; that there is plenty of work for all, and yours belongs to you and no one else can do it. It comes to you direct and the supply is abundant, and know all the time that this is so. Never let a lack of anything stay a moment with you. It is rank error and brings all sorts of disease and difficulty.

There is a continuous demand for all I have to offer. Neither malicious animal magnetism nor any erroneous mortal thought can hinder me from meeting those who desire to get what I have to give. No erroneous mortal thought, opinion or judgment can hide, hold or take from me those persons who can help, elevate or benefit me.

"I SHALL NOT WANT"

> I do not lack anything.
> I do not lack wisdom or love.
> I do not lack judgment or intelligence.
> I do not lack energy or industry.
> I do not lack and cannot lack anything,
>   or the means by which to acquire anything.
> I am not outside infinity.

My work is in Mind — it comes from God — it cannot be intercepted nor diverted into other paths, being governed by divine Principle. It is progressive, prosperous, satisfactory, joyous, continuous. It reaches from pole to pole, from ocean to ocean, perfect, infinite, going on all the time, for the glory of God. Perfect idea is already located with absolute satisfaction in Mind. In this perfect place in Mind, I am able to support myself, have all the recreation and companionship needed. In the perfect place of Mind is complete satisfaction. I live in the affluence of Spirit and am one with the inexhaustible, unobstructed, omnipresent source of income, and infinite as is the source, so infinite is the supply. It is the Spirit that profiteth. I am the ceaseless intake of God's eternal giving.

You, false claim of malicious mind, whatever or wherever you are, you cannot mesmerize me, or hypnotize me to think I haven't understanding to meet any claim that comes to me.

Money for God's work comes through us as His stewards. It is God, not man, who furnishes the means. . . .

We do not have to make money. God is our Father and He has all things, houses and lands, everything needful. If this is true, then man has them just as surely. He does not have to get them, he has them now, just as much as God has them.

(Mrs. Eddy illustrated this by saying, "If I stand before a mirror and pick up a book, my reflection does the same thing. It does not wait until I have held the book for some time, but picks it up at exactly the same time as I do, and therefore, has the book just as soon as I do.")

    You can demonstrate wealth. If you stand before the mirror your reflection is instantaneous, and just so you reflect God in all your ways. All are yours and ye are Christ's and Christ's is God. As a man thinketh so is he. Seek first God, and all things shall be added.

    Poverty is just as much a disease as cancer. Jesus says, 'Seek ye first the kingdom of God . . . and all these things shall be added unto you.' He did not say they were a part of the divine whole, but that they would be added. Our conceptions being yet material, the reward must come to our present consciousness. A realization of a perfect spiritual home will make our present home better. A consciousness of the purity of heavenly surroundings will bring out a more harmonious earthly existence.

    We tend too much towards the physical and this tendency produces discord. Jesus said, 'Take no thought for your body.' Do not let error tell you that you are not a good loyal Christian Scientist because you are not rich. The heavenward path is only won by struggling, but you will win if you faint not. If the senses lie about this life, they also lie about death.

We gather as we sow.

    My income is the incoming of right ideas. It comes instantly, constantly, continually day and night. It is my God being.

    Is poverty crying aloud in the land? Then we should know the purpose of God is rich in blessing to the poor — in Spirit. The fullness of the earth belongs to the healthful circulation of honesty, virtue and progress in the footsteps of Truth.

"I SHALL NOT WANT"

In her 'Science and Health' (found, signed, after she left us): Whenever there seems to be a need or lack in your experience, this simply indicates the scientific fact that this seeming need is already supplied by God's gracious abundance. Then give thanks with your whole heart because you have learned in Christian Science that God's supply is ever at hand.

Trust in God and He will direct thy path. God is beside us at all times and in our daily work. Realize the ever-present Love and rejoice. Error cannot rob us of our abundance; the demonstration of this is abundance of light and love and intelligence even for all our material needs. I CAN is the son of I AM because I AM is I CAN. I can express love, patience, truth, because I am. Declare against the sense of limitation and realize that nothing can hinder my progress in advancing and getting employment. There is nothing to hinder my success or progress. I am honestly ready to see what God wants me to do.

The Coin of Christian Science:
GOLD - The silent thoughts of Truth and Love which heal the sick.
SILVER - The spoken word of Truth and Love which casts out evil and heals the sick.
CURRENCY - The written word of Truth and Love published and distributed throughout the world healing sickness and sin. But this currency must be backed up by a gold reserve in human character.

Exclude time and place from thought — think only of here and now. Whatever is mine, is mine now; nothing can come between me and that supply — neither time nor space. Supply is, therefore, here and now. God cannot be impoverished; man cannot be impoverished. Nothing can come between me and my perfect supply; there is nothing that can take it away from me, for there is but one power, all harmonious, beautiful. I know poverty is an error that Truth destroys.

Remember, Jesus was a carpenter before he was a Savior of men.
Remember, God is the business man.

Truth does govern our business, and there are no failures nor reverses; God directs our business in Truth and the power of right thought regulates everything.

As malicious animal magnetism is only a false claim and really nothing, it cannot separate me nor anyone else from the best and greatest good, nor limit my supply in any way. It cannot touch me with a claim of poverty in any way in myself, nor in anyone, for Spirit is my unlimited source of supply.
I am not dependent on any personality for my needs. Malicious animal magnetism cannot hide my work nor blind my judgment, nor make me feel failure, nor lack, nor incapacity.

God gives to each and every one of His children abundantly all they need, and that supply is not — cannot be — hidden at any time by any mortal mind law or claim, for all laws and claims of mortal mind are false laws, and of the no-mind which has no real existence. It is destroyed by Truth now.

A Treatment for Supply

The power of divine intelligence gives you a business capacity without limitation, an acuteness and comprehension, a perception of character and clear-cut systematic knowledge which leads to success. Truth reflected by you attracts to you trade from all

"I SHALL NOT WANT"

channels of good. There is no fear, sickness, envy, doubt, anxiety, hate or jealousy. The discordant conditions of business have no power over you. You have no power to attract them. The divine Mind is yours to draw from and execute with, to bring out in your business harmony, success and prosperity. There is no unrest, discord, fear or friction; no weakness, discouragement, uncertainty or failure. You have an inexhaustible supply. There is no avarice, greed, trust in money, or love of money. You have abundant proof of God's loving care and His law of supply. You live in the land of promise. God has called you out of any sojourn in Egypt (in darkness), to return to your own country and inheritance. The days of hunger, famine, thirst are past. God is substance, Principle, Life. Man as His image reflects the capabilities and possibilities of Spirit. You live in Mind, in the atmosphere of plenty. There is no power or presence that can resist good or prevent your prayer being answered, from being effectual. While you remain in this frame of mind you are obedient to the Principle of your being and naught can hinder your healing the sick and the sinning.

Demonstrate your way out of wanting or needing money, and you will have it.

POSSESSION

by

Adam H. Dickey

There is a belief among mortals that they can become the privileged possessors or owners of something. When through the usual process of law a man acquires real estate, he has a strong desire to erect a fence around it and to keep everybody else away. Then follows the belief which is universally acknowledged, that he owns a certain amount of the earth's surface and that the law protects and defends him in private possession thereof. He builds a house and occupies it, calls it his own, and no one is permitted to approach or to enter it contrary to his wishes without being considered a trespasser. In our present degree of development it is generally understood that property is something which should have an owner; that the earth and all that is contained therein may be divided into parts and parcels, and that different individuals may claim possession of more or less of it to the exclusion of others. All this, however, is based on the supposition that matter is substance and that man is the proprietor of it.

Through the illusive processes of mortal belief, truth is apparently reversed; thoughts are externalized into things; and these things are claimed, held, and dominated by individuals. Some people have a large amount of property, others a little, while a great many have none at all. This apparently unequal distribution of material possessions fosters envy, jealousy, and strife, often provoking the one who finds himself deprived of his heart's desire into the use of questionable means, if not of physical force, to gain his object. It would be safe to say that nine tenths of all the war and contention in the world has been inaugurated and carried on because of the invasion of so-called property rights, or because of a desire to extend material possession or dominion.

Just as soon as a man finds himself in possession of a certain amount of matter — of houses or lands, of stocks or bonds — he is besieged by a sense of personal responsibility for his wealth and a fear that he may at some time be dispossessed of it. The whole system of property rights and of the division of property is based upon the supposed substantiality of matter, an illusion which some day must be dispelled by the law of God, which declares that Mind is the only substance. This change may not be brought about all at once, but through right thinking and conduct there will in due time be established the true concept, namely, that "the earth is the Lord's, and the fulness thereof." Rightfully speaking, everything in this world belongs to God, and through reflection belongs also to man, who is the image and likeness of God. When we have reached the point in our demonstration where we can resolve things into thoughts, the multiplication of these thoughts will be possible, so that every individual may reflect and possess all that belongs to his Maker.

In some lines of thought this ideal condition already prevails; for example, in mathematics. Let us suppose that the figures used in making calculations, instead of being accepted as thoughts, were regarded as material objects. In such a case every mathematician or accountant would have to provide himself with a supply of figures, which would perhaps be made of some durable material like wood or iron, and which he would keep on a shelf or locked in a drawer. When the mathematician wished to use the figures he would take them out, arrange them in their proper order, and be enabled thereby to work out his problems.

If in a busy season the accountant's supply of figures should become exhausted, he would have to purchase more or perhaps borrow them from his neighbor. He might approach a fellow worker and say, "I wish you would lend me two or three fives and a few sevens this morning; I am out of these figures." His friend might reply, "I am sorry, but I have been using so many fives and sevens lately in my work that I need all I have and cannot accommodate you." There might even be a shortage in figures which would affect the whole population, and there would be a scramble for a supply. The price of figures would advance, and if people really believed that these objects were a necessity, there would be such brisk competition that the price of enough figures to do business with would be out of all proportion to the cost of their production, and many people would have to do without them.

This condition of affairs, however, is impossible because of the fact that figures instead of being *things* are *thoughts*, and as such are everywhere present without limit or restriction. No contrivance of mortal mind nor any scheme of manipulators can take away from us one single figure or deprive us of instantaneous access to all that we can possibly have use for. No war has ever been declared because one nation has attempted to appropriate more than its share of the multiplication table, nor has any man been found guilty of using figures which he has surreptitiously taken from his neighbor.

Figures are not things but thoughts; they are mental concepts, and as such they are available to everybody. Sometime it will be realized that not only is this true with regard to figures, but that every so-called material object in the universe is but the counterfeit of some divine idea and not what mortal mind represents it to be. The time will come when mortal mind will abandon its belief that ideas are represented by material objects, and when this time arrives there will be no fear of loss of, or damage to, that which we understand to be an idea and not a thing. We shall then be able to realize what Jesus meant when he said, "Lay not up for yourselves treasures upon earth, where moth and rust doth corrupt, and where thieves break through and steal: but lay up for yourselves treasures [right ideas] in heaven, where neither moth nor rust doth corrupt, and where thieves do not break through nor steal."

You may ask what all this has to do with our present demonstration. A great deal. Christian Scientists may add to their peace of mind and freedom from responsibility by thinking along right lines and endeavoring to put into immediate practice the teachings of Christian Science. If a man is engaged in a business which he believes to be his own, of which he thinks he is the creator and proprietor, and for the success of which he deems himself personally responsible, there may be a great sense of burden attached to his position. He may suffer from poor business, loss of trade, or any of the beliefs which go with his particular occupation or profession; so long as he feels that the business belongs exclusively to him, he will never be free from some of the countless beliefs that are supposed to affect trade in general and his occupation in particular.

The remedy for this condition is for the man to begin to declare and to know that all is Mind and Mind's ideas; that there is nothing whatever about his business that is limited or material. If God is the creator of all, and if everything in the universe belongs to Him, then this business which the man calls his own is really God's, and the man becomes the master of it only to the degree that he conforms his thoughts and his daily transactions to the law of God. If he recognizes this, and applies his understanding of the Principle of Christian Science to his work, his fear and uncertainty will vanish. He will find himself conducting and carrying on business in the manner God requires it to be done, and he will exercise dominion and control over it just to the extent that he places himself under the unerring direction of divine Mind.

If a woman considers herself the owner of a home and that everything in it is hers; if she believes she has furniture and fixtures which are her personal property; if she feels that she has servants to manage and that she must assume personal control

Possession

over them as well as over every other household accessory, she may become so burdened with responsibility as to find herself utterly inadequate to control the situation. But if she is willing to accept God as the ruler of her household, to convert things into thoughts, and to understand that "all things were made by him; and without him was not anything made that was made;" if she can realize that divine intelligence governs and controls her servants, her house and everything that is contained therein, she will immediately lose all sense of care, fear, and confusion, and find that the divine law of peace and harmony has taken possession of her household and manages it. If she realizes that the servants are working for God and not for her, that everything about the house is designed to bring out and express the law of perfection, things will run much more smoothly for all connected with this establishment, and peace and joy will come to all who enter therein.

There is another phase of possession which is perhaps one of the strongest of mortal beliefs. Parents believe they are the privileged creators of something; that they can usurp the creative power of divine Mind and have children of their own, for whose bringing up, education, and future welfare they are entirely responsible. This feeling on the part of parents opens the door wide to the suggestion of failure, and the trials and tribulations which are supposed to go with the ownership and control of children assail them from every side. They must learn that God is the only Father and the only Mother; that man is the offspring of God; that he is not physical and material, but spiritual, reflecting and expressing the wisdom, love, and intelligence of infinite being. As soon as this line of thought is touched upon, the false sense of responsibility which mortal mind has placed upon parents is taken away, and they can then in the right way trust God to take care of their children, knowing that nothing can interfere with the harmonious results which accompany divine protection.

All belongs to God; nothing belongs to us. Man is neither a creator nor an owner. As Christian Scientists we can begin the realization of this at once, and the results will be speedy and satisfactory. But when we relinquish all thought of personal possession, this does not mean that we must sacrifice everything we hold dear or that we shall really be deprived of anything. On the contrary, it means that through an increased understanding that all is Mind and the ideas of Mind we shall gradually come into possession of all that is worth while. This is surely a more gratifying way to bring God into our experience than to cling to the old material illusions. The mere act of surrendering something is not in itself a virtue, nor is there anything to be gained by assuming a false sense of humility. It is true that there is much to give up, but it is always the old, unsatisfactory beliefs which we are parting with, and as these disappear they are supplanted by right ideas, which give to us a greater sense of freedom, power, and possession than we ever had before.

What did Jesus mean by the statement, "He that hath, to him shall be given: and to him that hath not, from him shall be taken even that which he hath"? Why this: that the one who has the right idea is really the one that "hath," and his possessions are bound to increase; while the one who has the wrong thought is the one that "hath not," and he must of necessity lose even that which he seems to have. What we need to do, then, is to change our method of thinking. Jesus' saying, "Seek ye first the kingdom of God, and his righteousness; and all these things shall be added unto you," is made possible only through Christian Science.

In *Miscellaneous Writings*, our Leader says, "Holding the right idea of man in my mind, I can improve my own, and other people's individuality, health, and morals." All things are accomplished through the *right* idea, which asserts itself in human consciousness and dispossesses us of our false beliefs. The only thing that can happen to the human sense of things is that it disappears in exactly the proportion that we apprehend the right idea.

It is a law of metaphysics that thought externalizes itself. Therefore the right idea in Christian Science naturally expands into expression and brings thought into a demonstration. When we attain the standpoint from which we can see all material things as beliefs only, and that these beliefs can be transformed and improved through holding the right idea, we shall then begin to bring into our experience the things referred to by Paul when he said, "Eye hath not seen nor ear heard, neither have entered into the heart of man, the things which God hath prepared for them that love him."

Another line of thought which suggests itself at this juncture, is that mortals believe they are in possession of a mind which they call their own, and that they can think and will as they please with respect to this mind. This belief leads to another erroneous conclusion, namely, that we are in possession of a body of our own, that we have personal eyes, ears, lungs, and a private stomach all of which we believe to be material, and for the well-being of which we are responsible. When this error takes possession of us, the next thing that mortal mind claims is an ability to deprive us of sight, hearing, etc., and that our stomach can become disordered or diseased. This is all the result of believing in another creator besides God, another intelligence and power to which we yield obedience. "Know ye not," Paul says, "that to whom ye yield yourselves servants to obey, his servants ye are to whom ye obey." The only remedy for the ills of the flesh is to correct the false beliefs that produce them by introducing the right idea. In *Science and Health with Key to the Scriptures*, Mrs. Eddy says: "Note how thought makes the face pallid. It either retards the circulation or quickens it, causing a pale or flushed cheek. In the same way thought increases or diminishes the secretions, the action of the lungs, of the bowels, and of the heart. The muscles, moving quickly or slowly and impelled or palsied by thought, represent the action of all the organs of the human system, including the brain and viscera. To remove the error producing disorder, you must calm and instruct mortal mind with immortal Truth."

In mortal mind's method of thinking, thoughts are externalized as matter and are called the body. When we understand this, and grasp what Mrs. Eddy teaches in regard to the externalization of thought, we shall see that our bodies are nothing more or less than the outward expression of our thought. Therefore, to heal what seems to be a diseased condition of the body, we must drop all thought of it as being material and recognize it as a purely mental product, an objectified condition of material sense, the correction of which, by replacing the false belief with the spiritual idea, will according to the law of God produce health and harmony.

God is the only creator, and all that He creates must be like Himself. Man is the individualized aggregation of right ideas, the compound idea of God which includes these right ideas. Knowing is being; "for God to know is to be." (*No and Yes*) Therefore what man knows of God constitutes his being, and the consciousness of man consists only of the knowing of those right ideas which already exist in the mind of God. It is scientifically impossible to put a wrong thought into consciousness, and there can be no imperfection in Mind since whatever God knows is perfect and inviolable and can never be changed or altered in any way. Nothing exists but God and what God creates; consequently there is only one right idea of anything. In *Science and Health* we read, "The divine Mind maintains all identities, from a blade of grass to a star, as distinct and eternal."

Mortal belief in its endeavor to see materially creates the human eye and declares it to be the organ of sight, while in reality sight is a quality of Mind, entirely independent of iris, pupil, lens, or other parts comprising the visual organism. When Jesus said that "the light of the body is the eye," he was not referring to a material eye, but to a mental condition. Hence what Mind knows about the thing we call eye is all there is to it.

This is also true in regard to what mortal mind calls heart, liver, lungs, and all else that goes to make up the so-called material body. Mortal mind claims that man is organized matter, but mortal mind's beliefs are not substantive, and the fact remains that the

Possession

only organization there is or ever can be, is that compound spiritual idea of which this material organism is the counterfeit. Inasmuch as there can be only one right idea of everything, there is only one right concept of stomach. It is not made of matter; it is not a material thing. It is a mental concept, and as such has its rightful place in the divine Mind. Any other concept of stomach is false and misleading, and must eventually be destroyed. "Every object in material thought will be destroyed, but the spiritual idea, whose substance is in Mind, is eternal," our textbook tells us.

It is time for Christian Scientists to stop trying to doctor sick organs and devote themselves to exchanging their imperfect models for better and more improved beliefs, which is the only true method of healing. God is the law of health and harmony to all His own ideas, and not only is this true, but the law of God which governs the perfect spiritual idea is also the law of perfection to the human belief of things, and this extends to every organ of the human system. Whatever God knows about hand, eye, foot, is all there is to know about them. He knows that they are not material, but that they are perfect, harmonious, and useful ideas, and that their identity is distinct and eternal. If a man has the wrong concept of hand, eye, foot, his only salvation is to get the right idea concerning these useful members. If his body should be injured, it would be his concept of body that is affected, not God's, and the remedy is for him quickly to give up his erroneous belief of body and acquaint himself with God's idea. "Acquaint now thyself with him [God], and be at peace."

In *Miscellany* Mrs. Eddy writes: "Neither the Old nor the New Testament furnishes reasons or examples for the destruction of the human body, but for its restoration to life and health as the scientific proof of 'God with us.' The power and prerogative of Truth are to destroy all disease and to raise the dead — even the self-same Lazarus. The *spiritual* body, the incorporeal idea, came with the *ascension*."

"I shall not want"

We can have no other body than the one perfect incorporeal idea. Man being the compound idea of God, it naturally follows that everything which is included in the consciousness of man must be spiritual and perfect, or it is not the consciousness that God knows and which man should have. Matter can never be spiritualized; but our mistaken belief which presents itself as matter can be corrected and thus spiritualized. To heal an imperfect heart, which is simply a wrong belief of heart, one must repudiate the testimony of material sense and claim the presence of God's idea, in order to improve his false concept. It is not necessary that he should know just what the divine idea back of the human belief of heart is. All he needs to know is that his mistaken sense of heart, which appears to be material, is not the right one. There is a right idea of God of which the human belief of heart is the counterfeit, and that idea of God is present now and here and there is no other. If a man has an unhealthy belief of stomach, the only remedy is to recognize the falsity of all that mortal mind says about stomach and claim possession of God's idea, which is the only perfect reality.

All sickness is due to a wrong belief of things, and the only remedy is to get the right idea. Because there is a right idea of heart and a right idea of stomach, we can understand what our Leader means when she says in the textbook, "Divine Science ... excludes matter, resolves *things* into *thoughts*, and replaces the objects of material sense with spiritual ideas." If there were no spiritual ideas with which to replace objects of material sense, our diseased beliefs could never be corrected and our bodies could not be scientifically healed. God is not separate from His ideas; the spiritual idea of anything is always present and carries with it the power and activity of infinite Mind, and when this spiritual idea is brought to bear upon the false belief, it produces a harmonious result.

If it is true that a wrong belief concerning body manifests itself as a disordered material condition, then the right idea which corrects the false belief must produce an improved physical manifestation. We can never heal by attempting to exercise the power of Truth on a sick body. It is the exercise of the power of Truth on a *belief* of sickness that produces the healing results.

Christian Science is an exact science, and as such it will permit of no deviation from its Principle and rule, It demands that the student, in order to demonstrate its truth, must be able to meet its requirements. Jesus said, "Ye shall know the truth, and the truth shall make you free." Then a knowledge of the truth of what Christian Science teaches is absolutely necessary to its demonstration.

We are all laboring more or less under the belief that man is a human being separated from his creator, with a mind and an intelligence all his own. This belief must be destroyed, and the only way to accomplish its destruction is by constantly holding in thought the right idea and by declaring the presence and activity of all the ideas of God. As these ideas become more real to us, the so-called human mind will disappear and we shall find ourselves growing more like Him, — more like infinite wisdom, more like Truth and Love. Then it shall come to pass as is written by the prophet, "The earth shall be full of the knowledge of the Lord, as the waters cover the sea."

THE LAW OF SUPPLY AND DEMAND

by

Lucia C. Coulson

The subject of supply is an urgent one in world affairs at present. On every hand we hear of shortage. Mary Baker Eddy writes in *Retrospection and Introspection*, "The first iniquitous manifestation of sin was a finity." That belief, of course, is at the bottom of every claim of limitation. When we see that in God's universe everything partakes of the nature of infinity, there is no place left for lack. Every idea being infinite, if there is enough for one there is enough for all. That must have been the way in which Jesus multiplied the loaves and fishes in the Syrian desert. He was conscious of the infinite nature of all divine ideas.

Now let us look at another aspect of this question — the law of supply and demand. Mrs. Eddy tells us that it is deific law that invariably supply meets demand. This fact should be pondered. First of all, it is a law that is announced, and law is that which carries with it the power of enforcement. Secondly, it is deific law, the actual law of Almighty God. Nothing can interfere with that.

And what is the law? That supply meets demand? Yes, but more than that. Supply invariably meets demand. What a promise!

To carefully consider this should change our whole attitude toward supply, for it means that whatever the need, the supply is there simultaneously with the demand. Suppose, then, that a lack or need comes into our experience. What comes with it? The supply. They are coexistent. If there is a large demand which seems alarming, what should we look for? The equally large supply that comes

The Law of Supply and Demand

with it. Let us keep our mental gaze on this positive truth. The trouble is that when there is a demand and we feel the claim of lack, we keep our thought focused on the lack, instead of instantly holding in thought the spiritual supply that is already there to meet it, remembering that the law of God is that invariably supply meets demand.

One cannot interfere with deific law and cannot stop it operating, but one must apply it to his problem and then trust its beneficent action. Seen in this way, demand and supply are one and the same. This thought is explained in another connection in the textbook, where Mrs. Eddy shows that muscles are motionless without mind. She says, "Hence the great fact that Mind alone enlarges and empowers man through its mandate, — by reason of its demand for and supply of power." Here we see that Mind itself does both the demanding and the supplying. Accordingly, if the demand appears humanly for a home or any other good gift, with the demand comes the supply. The demand is not to obtain something material from without; it is to appropriate something spiritual from within, because our textbook tells us that man includes all right ideas. If Mind demands and supplies power or any right idea simultaneously, we cannot be afraid of lack in any direction. Let us not be afraid to claim our birthright. Here we must be careful to remember that it is always a divine idea which we demand, and not a material thing, and that God determines the nature of its appearing. We must not limit God by human outlining.

Any belief of shortage arises largely from the false sense, or misunderstanding, of the question of demand and supply. Mortal mind with its so-called material world is the suppositional opposite of immortal Mind and its spiritual universe. Consequently, mortal mind asserts that demand and supply are always at variance.

If we apply the deific law, that invariably supply meets demand, to our own personal problems with good results, then we can do the same for the world problem, and we ought to do so. We are perhaps liable to be more mesmerized by the world situation. We hear so much about there being a deficit everywhere that we almost regard it as a fixed fact. But deific law is not variable, nor is it a respecter of persons. It works equally for prince or peasant, for schoolboy or the President, for the smallest business or the world situation. As Christian Scientists it is our duty to correct mentally erroneous thoughts expressed in the press or heard on the radio, to use our understanding to help the nations. The Psalmist said, "Give me understanding, and I shall keep thy law." It is through spiritual understanding that we are able to help and bless not only ourselves and our community, but our world.

SUFFICIENCY

by

Julia M. Johnston

The cause — God — which has produced the spiritual universe must have infinite resources for the eternal existence of its perfect work, laws for its continual government, power everlastingly to perpetuate it. This cause must be inseparable from its product, infinitely intelligent concerning it, and flawless in the maintenance of it. There must be perfection, also, of effect, if there is to be a perfect whole. Moreover, perpetuity of creation implies the orderly control of undeviating divine Principle, God.

Well may we stand in awe before the majesty of divine Principle, the perfect One, within whom " . . . is every embodiment of Life and Mind," all law, action, and accomplishment. All the qualities of perfection are expressed throughout God's creation. Everywhere divinity's boundless quantity is available and God's impartial law operative.

This cause, which is the Principle of all real manifestation, forms only perfect identities. With undeviating constancy it imparts to these identities the qualities of divinity, and governs their individual and universal expression. Sufficiency of supply is an eternal quality of God, and this quality is available to all creation at all times. Divine qualities cannot be accumulated or stored by creation, but they are being constantly expressed. Sufficiency of resources is maintained throughout God's universe by the operation of divine law, and so is present and permanent everywhere. Sufficiency of supply is not cumulative; rather is it being constantly un-

"I SHALL NOT WANT"

folded. Where the source is infinite there is continuous impartation, oneness of cause and effect, and no need for accumulation.

If in the universe of God's creating it were necessary for any part of this creation to accumulate some of the qualities, or quantity, of true substance, it would imply the possibility of a time when there might be an absence of substance, or a stoppage of its functioning, against which creation must provide. But such is unthinkable, impossible!

Divine Principle possesses infinite spiritual ideas, whereby it is abundantly able to manifest perfect harmony. All the ideas in the spiritual universe declare the control of divinity. In God's plan, man, whether considered individually or collectively, cannot accumulate or corner any quantity of substance. He can neither manage nor mismanage it. He can only express and be blessed by it. So man lives, not to accumulate supply, but forever to express its omnipresent sufficiency. Divine Science interprets through all creation the ever-presence of perfect supply and perfect continuity of existence.

Spirit enables all real identities to live within Spirit's resources, which are infinite. No part of God's creation can ever come to a situation in which there is lack. This truth is provable by anyone who will accept it and lean wholly upon it. Humanity may claim this truth today and experience deliverance from its belief of burden by the realization and demonstration of it. The divine law of infinite sufficiency operates with scientific simplicity, so that the supplying of creation with constant harmony is never obstructed or involved. Hence, the individual divine right and liberty of action of each idea is forever intact. Awaking humanity, beholding these ways of God, loving and obeying them, begins to be blessed by them.

Error, lifting its voice in contradiction of Truth, erroneously says, "Accumulation is the only way whereby men can be saved from disaster. If they do not accumulate material possessions, they will be helpless, hopeless failures." But there are countless ways

SUFFICIENCY

by which that, which has been saved, can be utterly wiped out. What a person has saved may even become the very means of his downfall. Surely such arguments as these contain no indication of absolute law, They rather indicate that the struggle for material accumulation may be part of the belief of animal magnetism which Mrs. Eddy describes in the textbook as, " . . . one belief preying upon another."

Opposed to this false belief stands the heavenly order of universal care, namely, the divine unfoldment of exhaustless resources. God has unlimited resources for His entire universe, and divine Science maintains the reflection of these resources throughout creation.

The foregoing statements, however, offer no excuse for humanity to be careless, extravagant, or thoughtless about what is humanly necessary and right to have. On the contrary, Christian Science teaches the application of these spiritual truths in human life through the exercise of wisdom, economy, and thoughtful provision for all entrusted to us by human circumstances. Spiritual understanding renders human thought more foreseeing, more prudent, more resourceful and alert. It causes all that is humanly done in accord with divine law to prosper and abide so long as it is useful.

Right investment of one's means may be as necessary as the right care of one's clothes or one's home. But let us not put our trust in matter in any form or amount. Rather, let us administer wisely what comes to our hand and abide satisfied in the understanding that Spirit is man's only real source of supply. Man's co-existence with Spirit enables him to receive the comfort, freedom, and support of infinite resources. If our thinking is governed by spiritual truth, all that is part of our daily human affairs, whether animate or inanimate, will be governed by divine law, and so will work together for good to those who love God — Spirit.

As humanity gathers the facts of divine Life through communion with the one Mind, and forsakes the beliefs of mortality, this process will preserve all that is useful and good in human experience, and will cause the evidence of good to abide and expand until there is no belief or appearance of lack left to deny the allness and omnipresence of good. We shall have far more to share by gaining spiritual understanding, and using it in demonstration, than we can possibly have by accumulating so-called matter.

Mrs. Eddy's life was a marvelous example of this truth. As she gave her whole life to the purpose of knowing God, for the sake of helping humanity, she became rich in spiritual substance; and this was necessarily outlined in her human condition. As she gained the treasure of divine wisdom, there accumulated a wealth of spiritual supply for her, and through her for the world. Mrs. Eddy writes in the textbook, "To calculate one's life-prospects from a material basis, would infringe upon spiritual law and misguide human hope." She has taught us by precept and practice that Mind alone is the Giver of all good to man. This spiritual fact is closely related to humanity's progress from sense to Soul.

Jesus had such a realization of immediate divine help available for present human need that he said: "Thinkest thou that I cannot now pray to my Father, and he shall presently give me more than twelve legions of angels?" May not this statement be taken as indicating that prayer to God, or the communing with the spiritual truths of being, is the means for humanity's deliverance from the sense of lack in every direction?

A familiar Bible story proves that the recognition of the spiritual law of divine substance, when applied in daily human life, solves its perplexing problems. It is the story of the widow and her sons and her pot of oil, which is told in II Kings 4: verses 1-7. Material sense, regarding the condition of poverty outlined in these verses, might have said, There are not enough resources in this family, so there must follow discord, disgrace, and sorrow. There is no solution for the problem. There has been no accumulation of matter, so there must be a time of punishment. Everything

Sufficiency

must express lack: the oil, lack of quantity; the woman, lack of faith and resources; the sons, lack of freedom; and the creditor, lack of payment."

But a prophet entered into the case. In the 'Glossary' of *Science and Health*, "prophet" is defined as "a spiritual seer; disappearance of material sense before the conscious facts of spiritual Truth." Elisha, the prophet, looked at the widow's case through spiritual sense, and he must have seen sufficiency as a quality of ever-present Life. Immediately the oil manifested sufficiency instead of limitation; the sons expressed assurance of freedom instead of fear of slavery; the creditor expressed satisfaction instead of deprivation; and the woman possessed further resources instead of poverty.

No time for the accumulation of matter was required. Mind was the multiplier, and sufficiency was made manifest even in the material realm, so-called. The false material sense gave way to the spiritual fact of Truth. Everything in the case, animate and inanimate, came into obedience to the law of God. Elisha's clear sense brought forth increased evidence of the exhaustless nature of true supply. He demonstrated the power of spiritual truth in the human problem. It is through such an example as this that thought is led to recognize, in every situation, that it is not the amount of material possessions which makes it possible for sufficiency to be expressed, but the understanding that sufficiency of good is a divine quality forever present and maintained by divine law; and this, in spite of how much, or how little, of matter seems to be present.

These truths are available for every human being to demonstrate. They can waken him to the realization that his situation is not hopeless, his burden not heavy, his poverty not real, his riches not uncertain, his possessions not fluctuating. In proportion as he understands and uses the spiritual facts of real substance, the good he gains is protected and preserved to him. Thus he will finally learn that God's divine method of impartation, and man's spiritual

"I SHALL NOT WANT"

ability to receive what comes from God, is the law whereby creation remains perfect.

Thus so-called human life will become an ever-increasing experience of awareness of the presence of divine truth. And soon there will begin to sing in the hearts of men the unbroken rhythm of the heavenly melody, "My grace is sufficient for thee."

SUPPLY AS SPIRITUAL REFLECTION

by

L. Ivimy Gwalter

Man has supply because he reflects God. The first chapter of Genesis states that God made man in His own image and after His likeness. Christian Science is the glorious discovery of the great truth, namely, that man is the full and perfect expression of God. Such being the fact, man has nothing underived from God, nor can he, as God's reflection, be incomplete or lack in any degree that which God includes. Therefore, man manifests supply, and, furthermore, supply is wholly spiritual.

The human mind challenges this statement. So imbued is it with the belief that supply is material, and that it comes to the individual through material channels and toilsome effort rather than from within, through spiritual discernment and divine reflection, that it seems difficult for the human consciousness to accept the statement that in reflecting Life, man reflects all that constitutes Life. Like the man in Jesus' parable who pulled down his barns and built greater, and said to his soul, "Thou hast much goods laid up for many years," mortals seek security in material possessions, only to find them fleeting, insecure, and illusory. Then they believe themselves to be in lack. Every manifestation of lack is but an illusion of fear, of ignorance, or of sin.

Spiritual supply flows directly from God to man; or more accurately stated, it coexists with God and man. It requires no human avenue or channel in order to be made manifest. Man in God's image can no more be separated from supply than he can be separated from God, for all that man has, all that man is, is the reflection of God.

When to human sense supply appears to be cut off or obstructed, either temporarily or permanently, when there appears to be no human source or avenue whatever through which supply can come, it will be made manifest when God is spiritually and scientifically understood, as witness Jesus' demonstration of the loaves and fishes. Man is not a channel for God, but a manifestation of God. He is more than the recipient of good; he is the expression of good. Man is not something through which or to which God flows; he is the very expression or evidence of God.

The love of money rests on the tyranny, the despotism, of materialism. It is that which says, "Without me — matter — you can do nothing, not even live!" Rightly considered, money is a medium of exchange, a symbol of gratitude, something given in return for value received. Instead of asking oneself, "How much money have I?" one would do well to ask, "How much gratitude have I?"

In its finite concept of supply, the human mind forever measures and limits that which it deems good and indispensable. Christian Science demands of its students a radical change in thinking. The sun does not say, "If only I had not shone quite so much yesterday, I should have more light with which to shine today." The fact that it shone yesterday is the proof that it can shine today. Yet mortals are prone to say, "If I had not spent so much yesterday," or even, "If I had not given so much yesterday, I should have more today." Such reasoning is based on matter and does not recognize Mind as the inexhaustible source of supply, and man as infinite reflection. Neither the good we did yesterday nor the seeming mistakes and failures of yesterday limit or darken today, except in so far as ignorant, false belief permits. It never occurs to us that the one who has passed beyond this plane of existence is cut off from supply, although every human avenue through which it came to him here is left behind. Neither can we be cut off from divine supply here and now.

Supply as Spiritual Reflection

In reality, supply has never been too generously shared, nor has it ever been squandered or unwisely invested. Being spiritual it is indivisible, and it coexists in its completeness with God and man. There have never been any mistakes or misjudgments in God's universe. Since no mistake ever really occurred in the past, it can bring no real consequence in the present.
Supply is man's today by reason of his relationship to God. He has eternal supply because he reflects God. No evidence before the material senses can alter this fact. In Truth, there are no lost opportunities, no past mistakes. Man is the present reflection of God.

If we would increase our human manifestation of supply, we must cultivate the habit of magnifying good. The human mind is prone to magnify evil; it holds to, recounts, and magnifies every disturbing incident. Alert students of Christian Science are seeing good multiply in their experience through the habitual attitude of minimizing evil and magnifying good. Which are we seeing — Love's abundance or error's want?

Strictly speaking, no one is ever without income. Something is coming into our thought every moment, either suggestions of loss, lack, impoverishment, fear, dismay, or spiritual ideas which acknowledge God and man's relationship to Him. We need to watch our thoughts carefully, for according to them the outward manifestation will be poverty or abundance.

Supply is not outlined or limited by the figures in a bankbook or the amount of a salary. Supply is as infinite and indivisible as God Himself. We must expand our thinking. Mortal limitations are self-imposed. Let us refuse to be mesmerized. In all God's universe there is no such thing as lack. No one can limit abundance to himself. Each can demonstrate it, and by so doing he is proving it to be a demonstrable fact for every child of God. We should not speak of "my" supply, or "your" supply, any more than we speak of "my" sunshine, or "your" sunshine. It is just sunshine, abundant sunshine, and each may enjoy just as much of it as he chooses, if he takes the trouble to go out into it, without limiting or depriving anyone else.

Human reasoning looks anxiously ahead and says, "At such and such a time my income, or part of it, may stop." God knows nothing about calendars, nothing about changes. Supply is continuous. The haunting fear of material supply and material lack will vanish before the scientific demonstration of man's relationship to God. In this relationship there is no stagnation, no obstruction, no unrequited, labored effort. Man reflects. He does not toil. Says the Apostle John, "Beloved, now are we the sons of God." And Paul says, "We are the children of God: And if children, then heirs; heirs of God, and joint-heirs with Christ."

Christian Science teaches that these truths relative to man's abundant present supply should be demonstrated as one spends or incurs obligations, for they are spiritual facts which it is our birthright to demonstrate. Such demonstration rests on honesty, purity, unselfish desire. Let no one think he can demonstrate supply in Christian Science for selfish gain or the gratification of sense. Scientific thinking is thinking that is in line with Principle. This results in a proper sense of values. It takes away both the love of material possession and the fear of material lack, for Paul writes, "Our sufficiency is of God." Mortal mind's lying mesmeric argument is always insufficiency. The one with the largest bank account may be the one with the greatest sense of insufficiency. In reality the only demands made upon man are spiritual demands. Mind makes them and fulfills them. Man reflects the infinitude of Mind — hence his sufficiency.

Mortal mind always begins from the wrong end of a problem in seeking its solution. Retrenchment and curtailment, while sometimes humanly necessary, never demonstrate abundance. The very fact of entertaining such a finite mental concept limits one's sense of supply, and therefore cannot demonstrate sufficiency. The position achieved through scientific demonstration can be held. There

Supply as Spiritual Reflection

is no reversal. There is no retrograde step. Error's argument is retrogression. Truth's command is, "Go forward!" This applies to finances, home, church, health — activity and usefulness in all their forms. Good is not attained negatively. Truth is affirmative. Principle is positive. We never advance through negative thinking. Christian Science demands that we keep our thinking positive.

In the Christian Science textbook, Mrs. Eddy writes, "Man reflects infinity, and this reflection is the true idea of God." And she continues, "God expresses in man the infinite idea forever developing itself, broadening and rising higher and higher from a boundless basis." As each individual learns through Christian Science to appropriate this truth, and grows in the spiritual understanding of God to the point where he can demonstrate it, this statement will be found to epitomize the permanent, positive solution of the question of supply.

THE DIVINE AFFLUENCE

by

Maria Soubier

The Bible includes many passages which present in metaphor and simile magnificent accounts of the affluence of God and His abundant provision for His beloved children. One such passage occurs in the fifty-fifth chapter of Isaiah: "As the rain cometh down, and the snow from heaven, and returneth not thither, but watereth the earth, and maketh it bring forth and bud, that it may give seed to the sower, and bread to the eater: so shall my word be that goeth forth out of my mouth: it shall not return unto me void, but it shall accomplish that which I please, and it shall prosper in the thing whereto I sent it."

To people living in the dry and dusty land that Isaiah knew, rain and snow seemed indeed a gift from heaven, a beneficent, vitalizing force that turned barren stubble into fruitful harvest. And thus did the prophet envision the culmination of the unfoldment of God's Word; it would not be sterile and fruitless, but would bring prosperity and plenty. Other prophets, too, caught glimpses of the glory that would attend a fuller understanding of Deity; but none knew how to demonstrate this affluence to the extent that Christ Jesus did.

In *Science and Health*, Mrs. Eddy writes of Jesus' work: "Through the magnitude of his human life, he demonstrated the divine Life. Out of the amplitude of his pure affection, he defined Love. With the affluence of Truth, he vanquished error."

Jesus saw that the general human belief is that everything is limited; but he knew that this was only an externalization of

The Divine Affluence

limited thinking. He knew that in reality nothing is limited. All is infinite, immeasurable good. In all of his work we may note this sense of affluence. The sick were not partially healed or a little better. They were made whole. To the emissaries sent by John the Baptist, Jesus said in part, " . . . Go your way, and tell John what things ye have seen and heard; how that the blind see, . . ." The blind were not given material aids to bolster up their courage; they were made to see clearly. Even in the early instance when Jesus turned the water into wine, there was not a little more wine; there was plenty. It was not inferior wine either, but, as the governor of the feast attested, the best wine of all!

In another instance, when Christ Jesus fed the five thousand, not only were all abundantly satisfied, but there were taken up afterwards twelve baskets full of fragments. Again, when the Master found Peter's wife's mother ill with a fever, he immediately recognized that the limitation of strength and health was only an illusion about her. In its place he realized the richness of her endowment. Her freedom was immediate. She arose and waited on them. Jesus' recognition of the divine affluence had healed the belief of fever and the need for convalescence.

On another occasion Jesus healed a case of lunacy after his disciples had failed. When they questioned him he pointed out that their failure was due to lack of faith and added that if they had faith equal to a mustard seed nothing should be impossible to them. What a faith-lighted thought is that — nothing impossible! And yet this statement coincides perfectly with the import of the first chapter of Genesis, where God is magnified as the only presence and the only power, the only Mind and the only action, and man is described as His image and likeness, the veritable climax of creation.

In the face of such amplitude it is natural that limited human thought should yield adequately to Truth. The student of Christian Science accepts this teaching of the affluence of God and makes it practical in his daily experience. When confronted with the argument of limited ability or power he knows that any limitation is illusion and that the measure of man's ability is affluence itself. He may remind himself that ability is an attribute of infinite Mind, an unfoldment of divine intelligence, and hence is immeasurable, always present, ever available, never subject to material so-called laws, unaffected by a cycle of birth, maturity, and decay.

Man, as the reflection of Mind, does not believe; he knows. In divine reflection, all the magnitude of infinite Mind belongs to man now as the reflection of this Mind. Mind knows all things, and man's reflection of this knowing is immediate. If the student's work along this line does not bring immediate results, he knows that he must press on until he perceives more clearly the true concept, the Christ-idea. Then the false belief will melt away. The true concept can never fluctuate or disappear. It always has been and ever will be, and it belongs to each manifestation of man individually through his reflection of God.

Just as affluence is the measure of man's ability, so affluence is the measure of man's opportunity. The glorious opportunity that is forever man's, forever discredits and is capable of annulling the belief of limited opportunity. Suppose advancement in business seems overdue. The student of Christian Science does not dwell on this sense of lack. He turns thought to the affluence of God's provision. He may remind himself that his true work is the business of being the image and likeness of God, a business unaffected by weather or locality, politics or season, depression or inflation. This true business is not conditioned by human laws of supply or demand, not subject to stagnation or reversal. The glorious business of understanding one's true self to be the likeness of Mind brings wisdom and foresight, perception and good judgment. The business of proving God's son to be the representation of inexhaustible Love is evidenced in abundance and generosity, comprehensiveness and bounty. The business of comprehending man as the proof of Life necessarily expresses unfoldment and development, expansion and progress.

The Divine Affluence

A man who knew something of Christian Science found himself confronted with the suggestion of lack on every side: lack of money, lack of a job, lack of clothes. He went to a Christian Science practitioner and had one treatment. His thought was lifted from the bleakness of material beliefs to the affluence of spiritual ideas. Immediately his human experience began to change. He was offered a job in a distant city, and transportation was provided. Thinking how much he needed, he suddenly thought of the words of the parable, "Son, thou art ever with me, and all that I have is thine." His consciousness was flooded with the radiance of Love, and he felt a glow of deep satisfaction.

Thirty years afterwards he recalled that never after that time had he felt a lack of supply. His business had prospered and continued to unfold in usefulness, and he had had the opportunity for membership and service in a branch church. He had demonstrated in his experience some understanding of the divine affluence.

Each individual's experience of the divine affluence depends upon his individual thought. His experience will be as good as his thought. As far as each one is concerned, heaven itself is fully demonstrable, regardless of what anyone else is doing. This fact is heartening to the student of Christian Science as he considers the problems of world government presented today. No one has to wait on others for the kind of government needed. Good government can seem absent only to the one who accepts the belief that it is absent. And when one rejects the belief that good government is absent, through his realization of the affluence of God's loving, beneficent rule he has proportionately evidence of more harmonious government.

Our Leader reminds us in our textbook, "We shall obey and adore in proportion as we apprehend the divine nature and love Him understandingly, warring no more over the corporeality, but rejoicing in the affluence of our God."

THE SCIENCE OF SUPPLY

by

Martha Wilcox

Some years ago a Christian Science lecturer made this startling statement from the platform: "It is a sin to be poor." Not long after this, a prominent Christian Scientist said to me, "There is no sense in so much lack among Christian Scientists, when they know what they do about the science of supply." And again, another Scientist whose experience and quality of thought was above the average, made this pointed declaration: "Insufficient supply is a disease, and as much so as insufficient health." These statements challenged my orthodox way of thinking. Unconsciously I, like many others, was holding to the old belief that a deprivation of wealth often developed worthy traits of character! I was holding to the thought that poverty and lack were virtues, when in reality poverty and lack are sin. I soon found that the average thought, in regard to supply, was indeed very feeble thinking. Like myself, nearly all Christian Scientists were "walking *into* or *with*, the currents of matter, or mortal mind," when it came to the demonstration of their supply.

We, as Christian Scientists, are entering this new age fully aware that we cannot escape the results of our own thinking. If we think "into or with the currents of matter, or mortal mind," we receive the results of such thinking, but when we think with our God-endowed dominion, we experience God's ever-present supply. We reap our harvest from the thinking which we sustain. Today we are where our thinking has brought us, and no matter

The Science of Supply

what our present environment is, we shall fall, remain stationary, or rise to new heights according to the thoughts we maintain.

The whole world knows that supply is vital to the well-being of mankind. As Christian Scientists we understand that fundamentally our supply already exists. We understand that the Science that demonstrates health, is the same Science that demonstrates supply. We are taught that every human heart can have its rightful need supplied, whether that need is one of loaves and fishes, or the need of tax money, as related in the Scriptures.

We who understand something of Christian Science, believe that the science of supply exists, is established and is as workable as the science of mathematics. When once we clearly understand that the character of supply is mental, as mathematics is mental, we shall have our supply at hand all of the time. We do not go outside of our own mind to get the mathematical value we need, and we do not go outside of our own mind to get the supply that we need. Jesus did not go anywhere to get the loaves and fishes. He turned at once to his own mind for his needed supply. Jesus knew that the loaves and fishes were purely mental; that they were thought forms, or forms of thought. He knew that each individual consciousness already included loaves and fishes and all other good as well. Jesus proved in this demonstration that we already are the infinite supply that God is being.

Everything of which we have been conscious, and everything that we shall ever be conscious of, even now makes up our consciousness. There is nothing external to or apart from our consciousness. Our supply is purely mental, and consists of infinite, divine ideas in our consciousness. These divine ideas are perfect and established, and make up our individual consciousness throughout eternity.

Infinite good is the all of each of us, just as the qualities of the sun are the all of each individual ray of light. The Father said to the prodigal, "Son, thou art ever with me and all that I have is

"I shall not want"

thine." This can be paraphrased: "Son, thou art ever with your own infinite Mind and all that your own infinite Mind is, — is you." To be one with our Father-Mind, is to be Mind's presence, is to be the infinite good, which appears to us as all things.

When we understand that our supply is purely mental, and consists of ideas already within our own mind, we shall experience our supply of things without delay, without mental effort or labor, and without the sweat of our brow. Whatever may be our supply tomorrow, or next year, was our supply a thousand years ago. Our supply of infinite, divine ideas has been inherent in divine Mind — our Mind — from the beginning. There is no time nor distance between supply and our own Mind that is being our supply. Whatever seems to be "over there" as supply, is here in our own consciousness as an infinite, divine idea. Bicknell Young has said: "The time will come when Christian Scientists by the thousands will think with the profundity of the divine Mind, without process, and shall acquire the objects of their thinking without delay, and with the certainty of the divine Mind."

It does seem at times that the human being wants and needs many things. This is mortal mind's worst malpractice! In reality we are never in a state of want or need, because the infinite divine ideas in consciousness are already complete and established. This fact of our completeness forever excludes our needing or wanting anything. To want something, keeps us from having it! Since we already possess the infinitude of divine ideas in our consciousness, we cannot at the same time need or desire anything. When we finally overcome our ignorance of the science of supply, we shall find ourselves in possession of all things. We shall find ourselves secure, abundantly supplied, and satisfied.

Many are saying at this time, [1942], that as soon as the war is over, we shall have automobiles, and gasoline, and tires, and sugar, and many other things. But why should we wait until the war is over? The five thousand could have been fed later in the day, but Jesus saw no need of waiting. Jesus knew that everyone in that

The Science of Supply

company of five thousand already possessed loaves and fishes, as well as all other divine ideas, that very instant, by way of reflection. Jesus understood that supply was mental and eternally present as divine ideas in consciousness. Like the science of mathematics, the science of supply was a mental operation to Jesus, and by exercising this science, the loaves and fishes were at hand.

Mrs. Eddy admonishes us in the textbook to "Establish the scientific sense of health, and you relieve the oppressed organ." And we should likewise establish in our consciousness the scientific sense of supply, and in this way we relieve the oppressed condition. Therefore, we should keep on establishing this scientific sense of supply until the various forms of lack are spiritually healed. When we recognize that lack is merely a false claim and never an entity, we no longer fear it, and the complete destruction of the claim quickly follows. Supply is purely mental, and when we displace the sense of lack in our consciousness with the true sense of supply, this sense of supply which we entertain will be manifest in our human consciousness.

Our heavenly Father is ever conscious of abundance, and by the law of divine reflection, we can individualize this consciousness of abundance. It is a present spiritual fact that we possess abundance, and nothing can interfere with our expression of it. Having once gained this consciousness of abundance, we can never lose it, for it is the scientific sense of supply. Wherever we go, we take it with us, and should everything that makes up our present human sense of supply be temporarily swept away, our scientific sense of supply still remains undisturbed and will manifest itself.

Mrs. Eddy has written in *Unity of Good* that, "Jesus required neither cycles of time nor thought in order to mature fitness for perfection and its possibilities. He said that the kingdom of heaven is here, and is included in Mind; that while ye say, There are yet four months, and *then* cometh the harvest, I say, Look up, not down, for your fields are already white for the harvest; and gather the harvest by mental, not material processes."

SUPPLY

by

Ann Beals

Centuries ago a great multitude gathered in a desert place to witness the healing works of a prophet from Galilee. As evening approached, they grew hungry. As a climax to that eventful day, Christ Jesus asked them to sit on the grass, and then he fed them. Bread and fish were passed out — more than they could eat. And yet there had been no human provision for that occasion.

What did Jesus *know* that he could feed a multitude with only a few loaves and fishes? He must have relied on something more than blind faith in God's ability to care for man. Many of his healing works suggest the presence of a spiritual source of supply that is instantaneous, inexhaustible, and practical to those understanding how to use it.

Evidence of this spiritual source of supply is not confined to the works of the Master Christian. The Bible records many instances of the use of the spiritual law of supply.

The prophet Elijah relied on this law when there was a great famine in the land. He sought out a widow who was about to make one last cake for herself and her son, and he asked her to make a little cake for him first. Thereafter, we are told, her cruse of oil and barrel of meal did not fail them throughout the drought.

In providing for the children of Israel during their forty years' journey in the wilderness, Moses drew upon this same spiritual source. In Nehemiah, God's care for them during this trial is gratefully acknowledged, "Yet thou in thy manifold mercies

Supply

forsookest them not in the wilderness: the pillar of cloud departed not from them by day, to lead them in the way; neither the pillar of fire by night, to shew them light, and the way wherein they should go. Thou gavest also thy good spirit to instruct them, and withheldest not thy manna from their mouth, and gavest them water for their thirst. Yea, forty years didst thou sustain them in the wilderness, so that they lacked nothing; their clothes waxed not old, and their feet swelled not."

The twenty-third Psalm opens with the verse, "The Lord is my shepherd; I shall not want." Divinely inspired men of the Bible discerned a hidden universal law of supply that we do not understand yet. Their reliance on this law appears to have been a way of life for them. Their words and deeds indicate *a very advanced form of intelligence* which they used with the same ease and assurance as the scientific mind of today uses its knowledge of chemistry and aerodynamics.

The world has evolved far beyond the crude life of Bible days, and yet lack still plagues mankind. For many people, poverty is all they ever know. In this complex age, we need a more advanced means for providing for the needs of humanity than scientific technology.

Is it possible to explain these Bible miracles in a rational way? Can we know what these prophets knew? Can we use this knowledge to achieve the same results they did? Actually, such a breakthrough is now possible. When Christian Science is used to give a spiritual interpretation to the scientific discoveries of this age, we can begin to understand how this spiritual law of supply operates and how it can be applied to our present needs. All forms of lack can be overcome right here, right now, through an understanding of God as the source of all good.

Christian Science explains the spiritual and scientific basis to Christ Jesus' healing works, including the many times he met instantaneously some immediate need for himself or others. Through the Bible and the Christian Science textbook, *Science and Health with Key to the Scriptures*, by Mary Baker Eddy, and other works on Christian Science, we have available the same form of advanced intelligence that was used by the men of Bible days.

Concerning the spiritual law of supply, Mrs. Eddy reaffirms the Scriptural promise in her writings. In *Science and Health*, she writes, "The 'divine ear' is not an auditory nerve. It is the all-hearing and all-knowing Mind, to whom each need of man is always known and by whom it will be supplied." She also states, "Divine Love always has met and always will meet every human need. It is not well to imagine that Jesus demonstrated the divine power to heal for a select number or for a limited period of time, since to all mankind and in every hour, divine Love supplies all good."

In Christian Science, we learn that abundance, not want, is the natural state of man. Through this Science it is possible to be as free of lack as we are of sickness and discord, as we learn how to draw intelligently on the spiritual resources of the one Mind. This spiritual method transcends human methods and leads to the use of divine metaphysics for resolving the problem of lack. Actually, this spiritual method is already in use to some degree, as seen in testimonies found in the Christian Science periodicals.

In *The Christian Science Journal* of January, 1960, we have the following experience: "A new student of Christian Science learned the importance of obedience to God. Early in the depression of the 1930's, this man found himself without employment. Though he was willing to accept any sort of work and explored every possible avenue which might lead to a position, his efforts were fruitless.

"After many months, during which hope and discouragement seemed to alternate, he constantly held to the truth that his place as God's idea existent in infinite Love could never be taken away from him and that this place was teeming with activity. He was supported in this work by the loving help of a Christian Science practitioner. But the problem of unemployment remained unsolved.

"One day in a moment of weariness and discouragement, he declared aloud, 'I have tried my best to demonstrate right activity; I have tried to apply the truths of Christian Science in every way. I know that I am the son of God and that He loves and cares for me, but I am still out of a job!' Suddenly he realized that he was declaring a negative statement as well as an affirmative one. He resolved, there and then, that never again would the word 'but' or any similar form of exception appear in his scientific argument.

"This young student was led to ponder these words by Mrs. Eddy, 'Christian Science and Christianity are one. How, then, in Christianity any more than in Christian Science, can we believe in the reality and power of both Truth and error, Spirit and matter, and hope to succeed with contraries?' And on the same page our Leader writes, 'In Christian Science, a denial of Truth is fatal, while a just acknowledgment of Truth and of what it has done for us is an effectual help.'

"Awakened by these truths, the student reversed his thoughts of failure and seeming absence of good. Within a few days he was led to take certain steps which provided a most interesting and lucrative position in an entirely new field of endeavor, a position which he enjoyed for many years."

Another example of the presence of a divine law of supply is shown in a testimony by a man from Chicago, Illinois: "At one time, during the depression, I found myself penniless in a strange city.

"I'd gone with a group of sales people I'd made connection with. But we'd only been there a day when these men began talking about leaving town without paying the hotel bill. I couldn't go along with anything like that, so I separated myself from them.

"But I was penniless, so I went to the manager, and told him I didn't have the means to pay the bill, but that I would have. Then I went to the Christian Science Reading Room to study and

"I SHALL NOT WANT"

pray. I knew this was the only way I could possibly solve the problem. As I prayed for direction and guidance, the thought came very strongly to give. But I thought, 'I don't have anything to give.' That happened several times as I sat there and prayed. Finally, the thought of service began to come to me. Well, I turned that over in my mind until I finally saw how I could be of service.

"At one time I'd sold a piece of equipment used by hotels, restaurants, and stores — a meat slicing machine. It had consisted of over a thousand parts and I knew every one of them. In fact, I had a set of servicing tools right in my car. These machines were in common use everywhere, but in these depression times the merchants weren't prepared to ship them back to the factory for repairs.

"So here was my answer. I decided to make some calls and offer to service these machines. And I was received with open arms. Between three and five that afternoon, I'd lined up enough work for two weeks. And for two years after that I made a living in this way, covering six states."

These two men turned to prayer to resolve their financial problems. Although mankind has always prayed to God for help in times of great need, so often such prayers were not answered. But because of the more advanced form of prayer taught in Christian Science, these men were able to find a practical answer to their needs. These experiences, and many like them, show that there is a spiritual law of supply. With Christian Science, it can be explored, analyzed, and understood so that its full potential can be realized.

No one should have to endure a life of limited supply. Here and now, through Christian Science, we can begin to challenge every belief in limited good and demonstrate a more abundant life for ourselves and the world.

The spiritual law of supply does not lend itself to a quick or easy explanation, but we can begin now to gain some understanding of it and prove it in our own individual experience. To make greater use of this law, we first need to be convinced that there is a spiritual source that can meet our needs in a practical way.

The Fourth Dimension of Spirit

How can the spiritual law of supply be explained scientifically? It appears so mysterious that it seems beyond understanding. Prayer is intangible and mental, and loaves and fishes are tangible and physical. Thoughts are ethereal intangibles, and things are solid entities. To the material senses, the multiplication of the loaves and fishes seems super-natural. Jesus' demonstration suggests that a non-material cause produced a material effect; tangible supply apparently came from nowhere, nothing. Yet "nothing" cannot create "something." Until the dawn of twentieth-century physics, there seemed no way to explain how an atomic form could appear from nowhere. But now, by relating modern physics to Christian Science, we can begin to discern how spiritual causes can create so-called physical things, and how the spiritual law of supply operates daily to bless and care for us.

Modern physics provides the first clue as to the scientific basis for miracles. We can relate them to a spiritual cause because physics has brought to light a thought-dimension underlying creation. Until the discovery of this non-material dimension, the natural sciences defined the universe and man as purely material. A material interpretation of atomic structure and behavior deny any evidence of a spiritual cause and effect. The physical senses testify to an atomic universe of matter governed by non-intelligent, material forces and laws. This creation seems to be a closed system of material cause and effect, complete within itself and void of any spiritual element. When miracles occur in this system, they suggest that God has briefly interfered with natural laws and somehow imposed supernatural effects on a material universe.

"I SHALL NOT WANT"

We have *assumed* that material causes produce a material universe. Actually, no final material cause has ever been established for the atoms and their behavior. Modern physics has instead pressed through the atom and discovered another dimension to the universe, one that is wholly non-material. This dimension appears to be the final cause for creation, and it is mental or spiritual. If this is so, then it explains how "something" can apparently come from "nothing."

The discovery of a thought-dimension to creation is of great importance in establishing a spiritual law of supply. The two testimonies that were given previously are evidence that the human mind is beginning to explore this law and make it practical. Although these men relied on it more through religious faith rather than scientific understanding, the very fact that they even knew about it and understood Christian Science enough to demonstrate it is significant. But to find a rational or enlightened explanation for these demonstrations, we need to intelligently relate the physical universe to the spiritual dimension.

To do this, it will help if we make a very brief review of the scientific events that have brought us to the edge of this new dimension and opened up the present age of metaphysics. The appearance of this thought-dimension is the result of a scientific revolution that has been taking place for over three hundred years. If we go back to the 1600's, we find the scientific age just dawning. Knowledge in the Christian world was a mixture of the philosophical culture of the ancient Greco-Roman civilization and the theological teachings of the Roman Catholic Church.

"Scientific" discussions centered on how many angels could dance on the end of a pin and whether God could make a rock so heavy that He couldn't lift it Himself. The creation of all things was set at 4004 B.C., at which time the universe was completed in seven days. There was a strange mixture of science and sorcery called alchemy, in which men believed that gold and youth could be

Supply

found through the proper mixture of air, water, fire, and earth. These concepts were fixed in men's minds as truth. This crude structure of knowledge was the mental atmosphere in which they thought.

At the close of the Medieval Age, a new mentality emerged in the Christian world. This mental awakening came from the church's insistence on the rationality of God, which suggested that the universe, as His creation, could be understood scientifically. The revival of the works of ancient Greece stimulated this scientific interest. Then Copernicus in the sixteenth century proved that man is not the center of the universe. He was followed by Galileo and Francis Bacon in the seventeenth century, and then Newton in the eighteenth century. These men and many others began lifting humanity out of superstition and darkness into the light of a scientific age. They discovered a *scientific dimension* to the universe.

There was order and plan in creation — so much so that the universe soon began to resemble a giant clock. It was so functional and predictable that a mechanistic philosophy began to replace theological views. Philosophers reasoned that once creation had been set into motion, it ran automatically through the action and reaction of billiard-ball atoms on each other. This theory seemed to fit all the discoveries of that age. This materialistic viewpoint became so complete as to be unanswerable. It was a concrete structure of so-called intelligence entrenched as truth in the rational minds of the nineteenth century.

With twentieth century physics, this materialistic concept was washed away in a tidal wave of new discoveries about the atom. Albert Einstein, Lord Ernest Rutherford, Neils Bohr, Sir James Jeans, Sir Arthur Eddington and others discovered that the universe is made of "mind-stuff." As they probed deeper and deeper into the secrets of the atom, the solid mass of the universe vanished into a non-material essence. The atom became a system of superimposed waves of energy — nothing more. Gradually, we have learned that all matter is made of waves of energy, and we live in a universe of non-material forces. *There is no matter as we think of it — no solid, hard, weighty mass impervious to the influence of thoughts and feelings.* In the last analysis, atomic form has no more solid substance than an idea or an emotion.

Where does this non-material atomic energy originate? Sir James Jeans was among the first to suggest, in his book, *Physics and Philosophy*, "a substratum below space and time in which the springs of events are concealed."

Lincoln Barnett wrote in his book, *The Universe and Dr. Einstein*, "Yet the fundamental mystery remains. The whole march of science toward the unification of concepts — the reduction of all matter to elements and then to a few types of particles, the reduction of 'forces' to the single concept 'energy', and then the reduction of matter *and* energy to a single basic quantity — leads still to the unknown. The many questions merge into one, to which there may never be an answer: what is the essence of this mass-energy substance, what is the underlying stratum of physical reality which science seeks to explore?"

Scientists are learning that creation is too complicated to be the effect of material causes, and this new dimension is assuming spiritual qualities. It is being suggested that we live in a universe of intelligence, with an underlying cause that thinks, creates, programs, plans, and governs all that exists. Einstein called this unknown cause "a superior reasoning power."

We see, then, how the thought image of a mechanical universe, contrived to fit the first scientific discoveries, has gradually yielded to the possibility of a universe with a thought dimension of infinite depth and meaning. It grows increasingly certain that creation can never be understood through laws of physics and biology. Rather, this dimension of thought-forces is revealing itself to be the intelligent cause of all that exists.

This thought-dimension is inseparable from all atomic structure and behavior. It would appear that every atom in the universe is completely controlled by the intelligence and power in this hidden realm. The atomic universe is made of elements that are no more solid than a thought or a feeling. The non-material waves of atomic action and form are emerging from a thought dimension containing mental qualities far superior to our own.

Because there is nothing material in the atom, atomic form and behavior can be defined as non-material or mental in essence. Since there is no material hardness to the atom, the atom is the same non-material substance as the thought-forces of the thought dimension beneath it. They are both void of solid matter. Therefore, atoms, individually and collectively, offer no barrier, no obstruction, no resistance to the control of the thought-forces in this hidden dimension. We could say that the thought-forces of the unseen dimension are cause, and all atomic structure and behavior are effect. This suggests that creation is not a closed system of material cause and effect, but a closed system of non-material cause and effect. To the material senses, the ultimate cause of all things seems to disappear into some mysterious, intangible realm that is non-material. To the spiritually enlightened senses, however, it would seem, inversely, that all things emerge from a spiritual dimension infinitely creative and intelligent. The spiritual realm of Mind originates and images forth, as atomic form and action, all visible form and substance.

We have, then, an atomic universe emerging out of a non-material dimension or spiritual cause that creates and governs the universe and man. As the physical sciences press against this new realm, its structure and contents remain a mystery because the material mind cannot understand it. It can only be defined in spiritual terms.

When Christian Science is used to define the nature of this new dimension, it becomes transparent. Its structure, qualities, laws, and contents are clearly defined in Mrs. Eddy's divinely inspired revelation of it. The thought-forces controlling atomic behavior are not physical or mental, but spiritual, divine, holy, Godlike. In

Miscellaneous Writings, Mrs. Eddy states: "Atomic action is Mind, not matter. It is neither the energy of matter, the result of organization, nor the outcome of life infused into matter: it is the infinite Spirit, Truth, Life, defiant of error or matter."

In this statement, Mrs. Eddy links all atomic action to Mind or God. In *Science and Health* she defines God as, "The great I AM, the all-knowing, all-seeing, all-acting, all-wise, all-loving, and eternal; Principle; Mind; Soul; Spirit; Life; Truth; Love; all substance; intelligence." Thus, Christian Science carries the line of reasoning concerning this dimension beyond human theories into divine understanding and anchors it on the same bedrock of Truth found in the Scriptures.

Spiritual Dimension Defined in Christian Science

Consider the potential that lies in the discovery of this nonmaterial dimension when it is coupled with Mrs. Eddy's revelation of its spiritual qualities and laws. Since the dawn of the scientific age, man's mind has been emerging from ignorance and superstition, pressing against the mental limitations within, shedding its materialism like a dark dream, emerging into the light, and moving ever closer to the spiritual reality of all things. Man had to pass *through* the scientific age before he could discover and establish as scientific fact the actual existence of a spiritual dimension in the universe.

With this mighty evolution, only the human mind has been changing. The universe is always the same. The spiritual dimension has always been here, whether men knew of it or not. It is possible that the miracles of Bible days were performed because the early prophets and disciples discerned the presence of this spiritual realm as a reality. They intuitively knew its divine elements and its potential to bless man. They utilized its healing power.

Supply

These divinely gifted men walked the same earth we do. They saw the same sunny days, the same starlit nights. They watched the flowers unfold, and they heard the birds sing. But inwardly, they saw it differently. They lived in a thought-dimension unlike that of the rest of humanity. Their works were not the result of faith or superstition. They knew exactly what they were doing when they met human needs with spiritual resources. They tried to define the nature of this spiritual realm, to explain how near it is to man, how tenderly it cares for him in every way. They proved by their mighty works that this dimension is not a cold, inanimate sphere filled with harsh material forces. It is "the secret place of the most high" — the realm of God. Although they provided proof that this realm exists, they lived too soon in the development of civilization to define it in such a way that others could understand it.

Christ Jesus foretold the coming of the full revelation of the realm of Mind when he promised his followers, "I will pray the Father, and He shall give you another comforter, that He may abide with you forever . . . the comforter, which is the Holy Ghost, whom the Father will send in my name, he shall teach you all things, and bring to your remembrance whatsoever I have said to you."

For almost two thousand years humanity waited for the Comforter that would reveal the secrets of Jesus' magnificent works. Human intellect and reason could not discover its nature. It could be explained only through divine metaphysics. Then in 1866 Mrs. Eddy discovered Christian Science, and gave to the world the first accurate and complete insight into this intangible dimension so hidden from the five senses. This Science is both a religious and a scientific breakthrough. Mrs. Eddy saw through the physical universe into this infinite underlying realm of Mind. Like John, she saw a new heaven and a new earth. In *Retrospection and Introspection*, she wrote of her first experience in discovering the dimension of Spirit, "The divine hand led me into a new world of light and Life, a fresh universe — old to God but new to His 'little one'."

"I SHALL NOT WANT"

Those who discern this spiritual dimension in its entirety experience a spiritualization of thought that transforms their view of creation. They understand God as the universal source of all good, as the one Mind creating and sustaining all things.

Two Viewpoints

In her writings, Mrs. Eddy does not tell us that there are two creations — one material and the other spiritual. She says there are two *viewpoints* — one material and the other spiritual. Throughout her works, she strives to separate these two views and to show that one is real and the other is unreal. In *Science and Health*, she writes, "The heavens and earth to one human consciousness, that consciousness which God bestows, are spiritual, while to another, the unillumined mind, the vision is material."

Christian Science reveals that we are not striving to reach a spiritual state of being somewhere in space and time. We are here and now spiritual. We are already in the spiritual universe here and now. Erring material beliefs alone blind us to this fact. To the material mentality, to the false, godless view, atomic action is harsh, cold, non-intelligent, governed by fixed physical laws that act regardless of the suffering, deprivation, and discord that they inflict on the living. But to the spiritual consciousness, atomic action is a manifestation of God, whose thought-forces act only to bless man. With the discovery of a non-material dimension underlying all atomic form and action, and with the coming of Christian Science, we have established an invisible cause — God — scientifically defined and related to a visible atomic effect — the universe and man.

From this, we can begin to make practical use of the spiritual law of supply, for *we can press through the visible world into the dimension that creates and governs all atomic form and action.* The one Mind, the divine Principle, Love, filling this spiritual realm, is active, creative, unfolding a dynamic creation and

Supply

supporting the life of man. The divine Mind and its phenomena, man and the universe, are inseparable as cause and effect.

God creates and sustains this creation through the divine law of supply. This law is manifested *through* atomic action and form. We interpret the visible universe and man materially, being ignorant of the presence of the spiritual dimension. But as we learn of the elements and energies of this realm, we see that God provides for His creation through atomic form and action. All supply is a manifestation of atomic form and action, and this flow of supply is governed by the divine Mind — not material forces. Because the atom is non-material, there is nothing in the physical realm to resist or obstruct the action of the one Mind. God is cause and supply is effect. God governs the manifestation and distribution of all supply.

The one universal Father-Mother God, the divine Principle, Love, has infinite resources for supplying all the needs of His creation. Unlimited supply is maintained in God's universe as divine law, and so it is present throughout all time and space. It fills the eternal now. All things exist at one with their spiritual source of supply. As a need arises, the supply unfolds to meet it. If infinite Mind has created the universe and man, then this Mind must be able to maintain them. Through atomic action, supply flows directly from Mind to man and the universe.

The law of supply operates in perfect balance with demand. It is never inadequate, lacking, out of balance, untimely, tardy. It is never withheld. It is practical, relevant to the very need where the need seems to exist. It manifests all of God's qualities, for it comes from God and must express the nature of its origin. Supply unfolds from God to all things, and nothing can be without supply, for it cannot be apart from God.

Man, as God's image and likeness, cannot exist apart from divine affluence. He cannot be incomplete or lack in any way that which God includes. Supply flows from God to man, and man cannot know lack for he cannot exist apart from God. God is inexhaustible good, and so divine supply unfolds perpetually in man's being, as his being. God supplies man's every need through a love that never falters, never changes, is never withheld. Abundance is the law of Love.

The material senses contradict this spiritual law, but if lack seems to be part of our human experience, it is because we do not understand yet how to utilize the spiritual law of supply that operates in our behalf. This does not mean the law does not exist as part of our life, but rather that it operates in a limited way. The good manifested in our experience at this time is evidence of the law of supply in operation. When this law is completely understood and proven, lack will be unknown.

Proving the Spiritual Law of Supply

These absolute metaphysical statements regarding the spiritual law of supply are promising, comforting, challenging, but in time of need, we must know how to apply them to our immediate situation with healing results. It is essential that we learn to demonstrate this law. Christ Jesus never hesitated to invoke this law in time of need. He told his followers, "I come that they might have life, and that they might have it more abundantly." He also said, "If God so clothe the grass of the field, which today is, and tomorrow is cast into the oven, shall he not much more clothe you, oh ye of little faith?" . . . "The very hairs of your head are numbered." Paul said, "In him we live, and move, and have our being." And Peter wrote, "Humble yourselves therefore under the mighty hand of God, that he may exalt you in due time: casting all your care upon him; for he careth for you."

Because the spiritual realm controls all atomic form and action, the one Mind can make manifest in our experience all the tangible good necessary to meet every need. God is here and now the Father and Mother of each of us — always present, always

Supply

caring, always aware of each need, and always ready and able to supply it.

How does God supply our needs? How does this care, this divine affluence manifest itself in our experience? It begins with the *unfoldment of ideas.* The resources of the one Mind are first known to us as right ideas individualized in consciousness.

We are accustomed to thinking that supply comes to us through objective means — that is, through the acquisition of tangible things *outside* of consciousness. Thus, we seem dependent for our good on conditions external to our own minds. But Christian Science shows that *the spiritual law of supply first acts subjectively through the unfoldment of right ideas within consciousness. As these ideas unfold, they move forth to be objectified as tangible good in our experience.* Because the realm of Mind fills all time and space, we are never separated from this inexhaustible source of ideas. Indeed, we are submerged in a reservoir of ideas that meet our every need. God, the source of all supply, is as close to us as our thoughts, and so the demonstration of supply begins subjectively.

Mrs. Eddy describes the operation of the law of supply in *Miscellaneous Writings*: "God gives you His spiritual ideas, and in turn, they give you daily supplies. Never ask for tomorrow: it is enough that divine Love is an ever-present help; and if you wait, never doubting, you will have all you need every moment."

When "God gives you His spiritual ideas," these ideas are inherently successful in their application to your needs, for they originate in Mind and are supported by the power, presence, and intelligence of Mind. They cannot be separated from Mind, but unfold under its unerring direction. They constitute your supply. The ideas that God gives are sound, whole, complete, harmonious, perfect. Because they come under the direct control of God, there is no uncertainty in the workability of these ideas, or the good they are intended to unfold. They are established by the one Mind as

"I SHALL NOT WANT"

answers to your needs, and they always accomplish the purpose He has for them.

We can compare the universal Mind, supplying all right ideas to man, to the principle of mathematics in use by everyone everywhere. Mathematical principles are applicable to every math problem from simple addition to the most involved calculations. Whatever the problem, the principle of mathematics can supply the right answer. The system of numbers is inexhaustible and never fails to solve a problem when applied with understanding.

Even so, the one Mind, the divine Principle, Love, is never without a right answer to every human need. However simple or complex the need may be, the infinite intelligence of Mind can supply the right ideas needed to solve the problem. These ideas are practical; they work. They open the channels of good that God has prepared for us.

We cannot outline exactly how this spiritual law of supply will work in each instance, for the application of this law to a need is an individual demonstration. The ideas that unfold are uniquely suited to each situation as it arises. There is a basic concept underlying the use of this spiritual law of supply and it is this: For every need we have, God has a way of supplying it. He does not know problems; He knows answers. He does not know lack; He knows abundance. He has a means for supplying the right solution or thing for every need, and this supply is immediate, practical, possible, irreversible. Whatever your need, you can be assured that the idea or tangible good necessary to meet it is already known to God, and it can be known to you as His child. As you demonstrate the ability to discern these ideas and use them, you overcome the belief of lack.

These ideas or solutions come to consciousness through prayer. As we pray for their divine unfoldment, we establish an inner rapport with God that opens the door to these answers. At such times, we lay aside all human planning, outlining, opinion, will,

Supply

desire, and decision, and in humility we yearn for God's will to be done. We seek His ideas, His guidance, His solution. When thought is receptive to the unfoldment of spiritual ideas and practical solutions, God then unfolds His answers to our needs. The inspiration designed to meet a need cannot be manufactured or contrived out of our own human mentality. Spiritual ideas are the gift of God. That is why prayer is essential to their unfoldment.

When a need arises, be assured that the spiritual resources are available to supply that need. It has been anticipated by the Father, and His answer is already known to Him, and it can be known to you. Then as you pray in meekness to know His answer, the answer will unfold to you as your own thoughts. If it does not come immediately, continue to pray and wait, never doubting. As you do, you will learn that God is never without an answer, a plan, a means of meeting every legitimate need you have.

God not only supplies the solution to your needs, but He provides everything required to fulfill the unfoldment of His ideas. He supplies the resources needed, and the necessary channels for bringing this good to you. If you have demonstrated the ideas that bring supply, then the action of Truth can dissolve all barriers, remove all obstacles, and change all circumstances that claim to obstruct the fulfillment of these ideas as concrete good in your experience.

As these ideas are manifested in actual experience, they are complete, lacking nothing. Every detail, everything necessary for their fulfillment, has been anticipated and supplied by the Father. These ideas bless everyone. We cannot demonstrate our own supply to the detriment of others. The manifestation of good that is ours does not rob others of their good, but bestows good on everyone.

How effective is such prayer? The following experience illustrates how such prayer works. It was taken from the *Christian Science Sentinel* of February 27, 1954. A man writes, "As the true concept of employment becomes firmly established in one's understanding, rewarding employment appears in his experience.

"This was proved to a student of Christian Science who, several years ago, stood in one of the crowded business sections of a large city sorely tried by the false belief that his God-given talents were unwanted and no longer usable. These suggestions of lack had resulted in alternate periods of apathetic resignation, or 'do-nothingness,' and frantic, aimless wanderings from one employment agency to another. The student silently turned to God and humbly prayed that he be shown the way out of the enshrouding gloom. Suddenly an angel thought came to him, 'Go to the books. Do not anxiously seek employment, but seek first to know the established fact that you are actually now employed.'

"Obediently the student turned to the books — the Bible and Mrs. Eddy's divinely inspired writings. There he learned that only the real man is the image of Love, the perfect idea of God. He discerned that man reflects the one infinite consciousness, God, good, and therefore that he is never outside of good or without it. He perceived that his previous thinking had been unavailing because it was based upon a false premise of an incomplete mortal waiting for something to come to him. He realized that God's sons and daughters, His spiritual ideas, always include all that is needful and satisfying.

"The student reasoned further that man has never been subject to a waiting period, past or future, and he rejected mentally all such aggressive and depressing suggestions as, 'A good job takes a while to find,' or, 'I've been out of work for a long time.' He saw that if the expectation of good is coupled with a belief of its postponement, it is a subtle deterrent to well-being, and he recognized that one should expect good to be demonstrated now. After several days of consecrated, prayerful effort his thought was illumined, and fear, self-pity, and self-condemnation were replaced with serenity, true courage, and assurance. Almost immediately, he received a telephone call from an entirely unexpected source offering him a fine and rewarding position, which he accepted."

This healing is an example of the power of prayer to overcome lack. It is an illustration of man's first breakthrough in discovering and using the spiritual law of supply in his own behalf. It indicates the infinite potential for good waiting to be realized on a universal scale through intelligent use of this divine law of supply.

What Causes Lack?

If the spiritual source of supply is so readily available, why should anyone be in lack? What obstructs the unfoldment of spiritual ideas?

Recall that Mrs. Eddy defines *two* viewpoints — the spiritual and the material. The material view is based on matter and its laws, material cause and effect, mortal life, and the power and reality of evil or animal magnetism. This false view denies the presence of a spiritual dimension. This mental state substitutes a false material concept for the real one.

Through this false view, man appears to live as a tiny speck in an immense world outside himself that he does not understand and cannot control. Through this inverted image, he sees lack as due to causes *external* to his own consciousness. Want is blamed on environment, weather, shortage of resources, fluctuating economy, governmental laws and regulations, racial discrimination, unemployment, inflation, age, lack of education, accidents, sickness — every kind of adverse circumstance. So aggressive and prolific are the reasons for lack that everyone accepts it as inevitable.

Men believe that lack exists because matter itself is limited and unevenly distributed. They believe that the universe and man are created and controlled by material forces, and therefore they are at the mercy of limitation, fate, chance, luck, circumstances. Because men have believed in the power and reality of matter over the centuries, they have experienced lack and limitation.

"I SHALL NOT WANT"

As we study Christian Science, we learn that lack is not caused by external conditions. All lack and limitation is in us — in this false material view we image forth as our life. Lack does not originate in matter. It comes from the hypnotic suggestions of the antichrist or animal magnetism, mesmerizing us into believing that matter is real, that physical cause and effect determine our standard of living, that life is always at the mercy of material laws which act regardless of the limitation and suffering they impose on the living. These aggressive mental suggestions obstruct and prevent the unfoldment of ideas that bring us our supply. These suggestions appear subjectively, just as God's ideas appear subjectively, and they are then imaged forth as limited and discordant conditions.

At the heart of this mortal, limited view is the "philosophy of the serpent" — evil's hatred of the Christ consciousness and its determination to control mankind through the lie of life in matter. This negative philosophy claims that matter limits and denies man his right to every good thing. Animal magnetism uses matter as a subterfuge to prevent us from detecting and rejecting the real cause of lack, — evil's hypnotic suggestions subjectively mesmerizing us. So long as we believe matter to be real and blame our limitations on causes external to consciousness, we remain mentally imprisoned in the false mental images of mortal mind. We believe that matter is limited and, because we depend on it, our supply is limited.

These illusions produce fear, worldliness, materialism, greed, jealousy, emulation, envy, selfishness, resentment, self-will, self-seeking, self-pity, inadequacy, frustration, limited intelligence, unfulfilled talents and skills, and many other false traits and emotions. These mortal elements in consciousness paralyze the flow of spiritual ideas, and thus produce lack. Without spiritualization of thought, this mortal, material state of consciousness seems to regulate supply and impose varying degrees of limitation on us throughout our lifetime.

Supply

Evil's hypnotic suggestions thwart and obstruct the manifestation of God's good in our lives. The limitation that we experience seems imposed by external causes, and we submit to it. As long as we believe that lack is objective, coming to us through external causes, we leave untouched the real cause — the hypnotic suggestions of lack coming to the inner self from animal magnetism.

To the darkened, materialistic mind, there seems to be only human means to turn to in time of need — human reason, intellect, opinion, methods, plan, action, will, work, experience. When these are insufficient to meet our needs, we seem to be the unfortunate victims of circumstances. We are mentally handled by the aggressive suggestions of limitation, struggle, toil, and want. The full potential of life is crippled by the unrelieved conviction that we are held down by stringent material circumstances.

If lack were due to causes external to our thinking, we would be at the mercy of material causes. The universal forces of matter would be too overwhelming and our individual Pefforts too small to effect a real and lasting change in our supply through prayer. But lack is nothing more than our own mortal thoughts objectified. We experience want because these mortal thoughts have become solid convictions in consciousness, shutting out the ideas that bring abundance.

However, we learn in Christian Science that there is no matter. In the light of divine metaphysics, matter disappears as the spiritual dimension emerges as the one cause. If Mind, God, fills this dimension as the only cause, and this one cause creates and governs all atomic action and form, there is no place left for matter and its laws to exist.

Christian Science overcomes the belief of life in matter and destroys these hypnotic suggestions of animal magnetism. Through divine metaphysics, we find that matter is a hypnotic suggestion of animal magnetism solidified into concrete conviction. It is the most hardened state of mental illusion put forth by the antichrist.

"I SHALL NOT WANT"

This mental obstruction exists wholly *within* consciousness, for actually there is no matter, only an erring viewpoint. All lack is hypnotically suggested to us as our own thinking. Because we do not know that lack originates in evil, we believe these false concepts and project these thought images outwardly as chronic lack.

So long as man strives to overcome lack through human effort and means, he will fail to do so. Lack does not originate in his environment, but in the hypnotic suggestions originating in animal magnetism, coming to him as his own thoughts. These aggressive mental suggestions will never be destroyed through material or human efforts. They can only be overcome through a spiritual understanding of God and man in His likeness.

Lack is limited thinking, a dearth of spiritual ideas, due to an acceptance of the universal material viewpoint. When thought is filled with material, mortal elements, we must toil and struggle to satisfy our needs. When thought is filled with spiritual ideas, the flow of thought is effortless, and supply is more abundant and easily attained, even spontaneous at times. The more solid our convictions of the reality of matter and evil, the more the belief and fear of lack controls our being. The more solid our convictions of Truth, the more abundant the good in our life.

Unless the inner self is actually treated for the mesmeric belief of lack, this specific error can cling stubbornly to our mental-makeup for a lifetime, causing the level of supply to remain basically the same year after year. So long as we believe that our supply is governed by causes outside of consciousness, to that degree will animal magnetism control our supply. We experience lack to the degree that we believe in it.

The same prayerful work in Christian Science that heals sickness and discord, heals lack. Once we begin this prayerful work, the mesmerism of the belief in lack begins to break down. If you seem imprisoned in stringent circumstances, you can be free of

Supply

them, for the infinite resources of the one Mind are always available to you to counteract this false belief, and you can break down this belief through prayer.

Consider the significance of this fact. It is not your physical life that is in lack; it is your mind that seems to be in lack — lack of spiritual understanding, lack of unselfed love, lack of trust in God, lack of obedience to His laws, etc. A mind clogged by material, mortal beliefs offers little opportunity for God's ideas to reach it. Increased supply is in direct proportion to the spiritualization of thought coming about through prayerful work.

Lack and limitation are in us, not in God or the universe. Insufficiency is a mortal belief projected as human experience. The demonstration of supply must first come to us from Mind, *through* consciousness, before it is manifested outwardly as tangible good. Abundance comes as we spiritualize consciousness and provide an avenue through which spiritual ideas can flow most freely.

We do not pray to demonstrate things, but to discern right ideas. If the right idea has unfolded to us, then it is a law that this idea must move forth and manifest itself as good in our experience.

When you realize that the law of supply first acts in your life as a subjective experience and is the direct result of Christian Science treatment, then this law begins to be active in your experience. However strong the mesmerism of lack may be in the minds of those around you, it cannot touch you or deprive you of the good you have demonstrated. The demonstration of divine affluence is mental — a thought action that takes place within the subjective realm of your own mind. It is solely an event between you and God. Therefore, there is no barrier or influence that others can impose upon you to deprive you of your good. As Christian Science is understood and lived, your supply is controlled by God, and must come in proportion to your reflection of Him. As you gain spiritual understanding, this must be manifested as increased good in your experience.

"I SHALL NOT WANT"

With Christian Science, we look *within* consciousness, see *through* the illusion of matter, and detect the hypnotic suggestions of evil arguing to us that we are in need, that we are incomplete, that we are at the mercy of matter. We counteract these suggestions with divine metaphysics. We see matter as an illusion and evil as an unreality. We exchange material belief for spiritual truth. There is no hypnotic suggestion so hardened, so chronic in our thinking, that it cannot be detected and destroyed through the unfoldment of spiritual ideas. However, it is necessary to understand that lack is not really overcome through human effort or human goodness alone, nor through blind faith in God's ability to care for us. Lack must be handled through treatment and its mesmerism destroyed.

This prayerful work involves two parts: first, affirming God's spiritual law of supply that unfolds abundance by operating through the unfoldment of spiritual ideas; and second, denying animal magnetism's aggressive suggestions that cause lack by obstructing the unfoldment of these ideas through the belief in matter and mortality.

Through your work with treatment, you can counteract evil's suggestions by knowing that you are never separated from the source of right ideas. These ideas are as near to you as your mind. Your supply flows directly from God to you, for you are the expression of these ideas.

As God's reflection, you embody every spiritual quality necessary to demonstrate supply: intelligence, creativity, perspicacity, ability, accuracy, wisdom, joy, love, integrity, honesty, right ambition, the ability to express unlimited ideas, and to live the law of Love.

The opportunity to develop your potential for unlimited good lies within yourself. As you handle animal magnetism's suggestions of lack and limitation, you de-mesmerize consciousness and begin to prove the spiritual law of abundance in your own experience.

Supply

Supply and Scientific Prayer

So far, we have seen that the law of supply operates through the unfoldment of spiritual ideas imparted from Mind to man; and animal magnetism causes lack by obstructing this unfoldment through mesmerism and aggressive mental suggestions. The change from the belief of lack to the expression of abundance involves spiritualization of thought. This means putting out the mesmeric beliefs of lack and realizing the unfoldment of spiritual ideas. This is done through the form of prayer unique to Christian Science — the prayer of affirmation and denial.

Healing of lack in Christian Science rests on a scientific basis. It involves three metaphysical laws. *First: there is the law that your thinking determines your experience.* Insufficiency may seem to be caused by external circumstances, but actually limitation of any kind is part of your life because it is first part of your consciousness. Lack and limitation exist as mesmeric conditions entrenched as solid convictions that are imaged forth in your human experience as want. Any mesmeric belief of limitation embraced in consciousness produces lack, discord, even sickness, and will not yield without persistent prayerful work.

Second: there is the law that your concept of supply can be changed through an understanding of God as the source of all good. You realize this understanding through prayer. The Christian Science treatment brings a healing renovation to the innermost thoughts as the spiritual viewpoint replaces the material one. As God's ideas unfold through prayer, they uncover and destroy the mesmerism of limited good. Through scientific prayer, you can change how you think. The change within is very consciously felt. You sense the letting go of old beliefs and the unfoldment of new ideas. You are aware that spiritualization of thought is taking place. Prayerful work can be applied to lack just as it is applied to sickness, disease, and every other claim of mortal mind.

Third: there is the law that this mental change must move forth and change your experience. As a more spiritual state of mind brings a flow of ideas, these ideas must be manifested in a more abundant life. True supply is evidence of God's love in action, of divine intelligence, wisdom, and affluence in operation. God is man's real and only source of good. He is the Giver of every useful, right idea. His ideas are never withheld from man. They unfold to you in proportion to your reflection of Godlike qualities. This unfoldment is subjective; it takes place always within the sphere of your own thinking. Your affluence is in proportion to the spiritualization of your thought.

As you can see, the key to having abundance is found in the second law, where the material view is exchanged for the spiritual view. Affluence comes through spiritualization of thought, and this is accomplished through study and prayer. The mesmerism of lack is broken through a consecrated study of the Bible and *Science and Health*, along with other works on Christian Science.

This study alone can change how you think. New ideas and fresh inspiration come as you meditate on divine metaphysics. This expansion of thought is progressive. That is, each day's insight into Truth builds in consciousness a foundation of knowledge about the spiritual nature of all things. This work destroys the many forms of mesmerism that cause lack, and opens the channels of thought through which the spiritual law of supply can manifest itself. This study also prepares you to pray.

There are many ways of praying, but the one basic to Christian Science healing is the prayer of affirmation and denial. In this form of prayer, you mentally argue for the spiritual viewpoint and against the material viewpoint in your own consciousness. You affirm the allness of God and the perfection of His creation, including man. You also deny the reality and power of matter and animal magnetism.

This scientific prayer can be used to treat lack as readily as it is used to treat every other form of discord. In this prayerful

Supply

work, you acknowledge the allness of God as the one Father-Mother, tenderly caring for His image and likeness, man. Affirm the presence of the spiritual realm as the source of all good. Recognize the activity of the spiritual law of supply as the unfoldment of right ideas to consciousness. Express gratitude for God's care of you. Realize that He knows every need that you have and has already supplied it.

Affirm the good. Expect God to care for you. Be grateful for the good that you have today — the groceries you purchase, your home, your work, your income, the help given you by another. The more emphasis you place on the good you already have, the more you acknowledge the spiritual law of supply already operating in your behalf here and now. As you do this, you come to understand and trust this law. Mental limitations and material barriers dissolve as you push against them and break them down.

In some instances, the mesmerism of lack is so strong that the affirmation of Truth is not enough to overcome it. In such cases, it is necessary to deny animal magnetism persistently and vehemently. Reject the entire illusion of matter and its laws. Destroy the hidden source of lack, the aggressive mental suggestions of matter and its laws. Christian Science shows the allness of God and the nothingness of evil. Challenge the mesmeric belief in lack with the fact that the source of all good is God and He is always supplying your every need. God's resources are manifested in your life as tangible good in proportion to the spiritualization of your thinking.

So long as suggestions of lack exist, they control your supply. Therefore, they must be specifically denied and destroyed. These mortal beliefs often demand a vigorous and repeated denial before they can be made to loosen, dissolve, and disappear.

Wrestle with the elements of fear, self-condemnation, self-pity, inferiority, worldliness, false ambition, materialism, jealousy, emulation, procrastination, laziness, apathy, conservatism — all the mortal traits that claim to obstruct the unfoldment of good. Reject

"I shall not want"

every specific suggestion of lack that presents itself to you. Stop mentally arguing bad luck, adversity, limitation, insufficiency, stringency, frugality. As you argue for abundance and against all suggestions of lack, these mental obstructions will yield to prayer and disappear.

In this work, you can analyze your thinking in order to detect and reject these false suggestions. Uncover the false traits and emotions that produce the belief in lack and heal them.

One of the greatest obstacles to the demonstration of better supply is *fear* — fear that you will not have enough to meet your needs, fear of the future, fear of economic conditions, fear that you are not capable of the spiritual understanding that heals lack, fear that God doesn't know your needs, that He can't supply them, that He has no way of bringing your supply to you. Every form of fear is hypnotic suggestion that you must handle with divine metaphysics.

Your trust in God to care for you precedes the manifestation of good in your experience. Implicit faith in God to support you enables you to relinquish fear, self-will, outlining, planning, struggle, and you begin to turn to Him for the answers to each need. Doubt, pessimism, anxiety, fear, worry yield to the expectancy of good, when you know there is a Mind outside of and beyond yourself that can and will supply your every need. Fear and selfishness give way to the humble acknowledgment of God as the origin and source of every right idea. This prayerful work dissolves negative beliefs and establishes love, gratitude, assurance, peace, quietness, and expectancy of good.

One basic cause of lack is the belief that we have a personal history of lack that goes back to our earliest memories. This thought-pattern of chronic limitation can affect our present circumstances. If this applies to you, counteract this by realizing that you have never been in lack, for you have never been out of the care of God or apart from His ideas. Any condition of lack, past or present,

Supply

is only hypnotic suggestion. Animal magnetism alone originates it, believes it, experiences it, and suffers from it. It has never entered your true being because it is unknown to God.

It is important to see through the thought-patterns of the past if you would not be trapped in stagnancy and apathy. These beliefs may heal slowly, but without this prayerful work, it is doubtful that they would heal at all. Reject a limited past, all suggestions that you do not have enough for today, all fear of the future. *Refuse to believe in lack! Refuse to be shut out of the good that God has given you!* Take a strong stand against the belief in limited resources until it yields to a quiet assurance that God cares for you and His care is manifested in affluence.

Every right idea that you affirm in your study and treatment means greater good manifested in your experience. Every false suggestion that is uncovered and handled by denial enables you to replace the material view with the spiritual. Every time you argue *for* the spiritual facts of abundance and *against* the illusions of want and limitation, you affect how you think. This prayerful work brings a *shifting* within, a *lifting* of negative thoughts, and an *unfolding* of right ideas. This inner change means that lack is yielding to better supply. Healing is taking place.

This truth active in consciousness brings about a mental atmosphere that is open to the unfoldment of ideas. Every spiritual quality within contributes to a state of mind that is a channel for the unfoldment of God's ideas. While we of ourselves cannot contrive or create the ideas we need, nor can we force them to unfold, we can achieve a spiritual state of mind through which they can appear spontaneously.

As your metaphysical work brings about greater obedience, humility, trust, gratitude, and unselfed love, there will appear this flow of ideas in consciousness. These ideas are spiritual, creative, intelligent, practical ideas, especially designed to meet the needs you have at the moment.

"I shall not want"

There are times when these ideas appear in consciousness complete and clearly defined. Then again, they may begin as small intuitions and grow as you pray over them. Sometimes ideas unfold by degrees; sometimes they are very different from what was expected. But if there is unfoldment taking place, if new thoughts are coming to you as you pray, then the law of supply is acting in your experience, and these ideas must move forth to "give you daily supplies."

Taking the Human Footsteps

When God gives you His ideas, you must use them. You should not substitute prayer for human activity. Prayer is used to gain ideas, enlightenment, direction, plan, and insight so that your activity will be productive and rewarding.

Actually there are three parts to the demonstration of God's law of supply. *First, the prayerful work that brings the unfoldment of ideas. Second, acting on these ideas. Third, realizing and accepting the supply that these ideas bring.* Sometimes, as we pray, the supply appears spontaneously as a result of the realization of Truth. But at other times, we have to act on the ideas that unfold to us, express them, carry them out, in order for the supply to come to us.

God unfolds to us only those opportunities that we can and will use at the time of unfoldment. Using those ideas or opportunities leads to the unfoldment of further ideas, when we are ready for them. The law of supply always operates in the area of what is possible for us to achieve within the framework of our present experience and at the standpoint of our present understanding. God does not force us beyond what we can prove, neither does He withhold from us what we have demonstrated. He provides everything for the fulfillment of each idea that He gives.

As you discern and act on these ideas, lack and limitation disappear from your experience. The supply of every need will appear as the need arises — money for necessities, right employment, opportunity and progress in your work, a better environment, greater freedom in your activities.

The immediate result of this work is not always huge sums of money and many possessions. Instead, you find in your day-to-day living, the unfoldment of everything you need in each moment of the day. The true demonstration of this law is freedom from materialism. The children of Israel were not burdened with forty years' provisions as they wandered through the wilderness. They were secure in God's keeping whether they knew it or not. Each day the things they needed were provided for them. Nor was Christ Jesus encumbered with many possessions. God knew what he needed and provided it for him at the time of the need. We see here the perfect balance of supply and demand.

Our supply is like a well. As we draw on it wisely, it replenishes itself. True supply comes through oneness with God. His law provides for us from His inexhaustible resources. As we learn to lean on God for all things, trusting Him to care for us, listening within for His ideas, we find that, day by day, everything we need comes to us. Nor is there any limit to the good we can have. The demonstration of supply is progressive. As we work to break down the belief of lack, increased good flows into our lives. God's resources are infinite. The good we have is in proportion to the spiritual understanding we demonstrate. Thus, our supply rests on a spiritual foundation. We can never lose the good we have demonstrated because it is the result of our solid conviction that the spiritual law of supply works and works eternally, for it is of God.

Summary

To summarize this concept of the spiritual law of supply: God is the one perfect cause, and man and the universe are the perfect effect of this cause. All substance, all atomic structure and action, is spiritual, not material. The atom is not made of matter as we think of it. It is composed of elements that are non-material — the atom has no more solidity than a thought or a feeling. All atomic action is governed by a spiritual dimension that is intelligent, loving, good, for it is the one infinite Mind, God. Because atomic structure and behavior are non-material and the spiritual dimension is also non-material, there is no barrier, no obstacle, no resistance between God and His creation. The spiritual cause is God, and the spiritual effect is man and the universe. Everything real must first exist as an idea in Mind before it becomes a tangible atomic form, and all that exists is possessed and controlled by the one Mind.

This spiritual realm is a reservoir of ideas or thought-forces that supply every need in the universe. To Mind there are no needs, no problems, no wants. There is only a perfect balance of supply and demand through divine ideas, intelligent answers and practical solutions to every need. Here and now, this realm is available as an inexhaustible source of supply to everyone.

Spiritual supply first unfolds to us as ideas — spiritual ideas, creative ideas, intelligent ideas, practical ideas. These ideas come to us through study and prayer. They unfold subjectively as we understand God. By praying scientifically, we put off the material view and put on the spiritual view. As we affirm the truth and deny animal magnetism, we purify consciousness and embody a mental atmosphere in which right ideas unfold daily as we need them. These ideas then move forth and manifest themselves as tangible good in our experience. God's ideas are not a substitute for human activity. They are meant to enlighten, guide, support, prosper, and inspire our daily activity. As we use these ideas, they bring us our daily supply. The more we spiritualize consciousness and express right ideas, the greater the supply of good in our life. As this spiritual law of supply is understood and used on a universal scale, lack and limitation will give way to an abundance of good for all mankind.

Supply

Testimonies of the Demonstration of the Law of Supply

The following testimonies further illustrate the practicality of the spiritual law of supply presently being used by Christian Scientists throughout the world.

In a *Century of Christian Science Healing*, a woman tells us, "The day came when I received my first contract as a costume designer with one of the big motion picture studios in Hollywood. Although Christian Science had been a help to me before, the desire for more and more money, more importance, more fame, grew in my thought, shutting out everything else.

"I spent much time and effort in pursuit of the people and things which I felt would make me important. I became resentful of other people's success, and began running around trying to do everything I could to get my human personality admired and sought after. I had my office painted shocking pink, and hired a publicity agent. I worked very hard to know all the press people. I would take them to lunch, and cultivate everyone I could think of in this line. I was in night clubs three and four nights a week, because I thought one had to be seen. My husband tried to assist me in everything I wanted. Now I realize he suffered patiently, silently, and quietly. This went on for about eleven years.

"When something didn't go right or I was pushed aside in favor of someone else, I would call a Christian Science practitioner and I'd get out a *Sentinel* or *Journal* and read a little until things quieted down. Then I would go on. I felt I was being very gay and sophisticated and I did everything I thought I wanted to do.

"When all my 'striving and contriving' failed to accomplish all I had hoped for, I decided to extend my activities. Designers who had their own businesses appeared to me to be very successful and sought after, so I decided that I must do this too. I opened my own wholesale business in better dresses with a big splash and for a little while I had tremendous success. Then the studio decided that my interests were divided, and they certainly were, and so my contract wasn't renewed, which was a great blow to me. The business was on such a shaky foundation that it had to be terminated, amid much bitterness. I was told by a great many stores that nothing connected with my name would interest them again. Within a period of about eight months, everything in my carefully arranged world fell apart. All of it just disappeared under my feet. Not only everything for which I had worked for years was gone, but my name which I had tried so hard to make important now stood for failure.

"I couldn't get a studio job, I couldn't get a manufacturing job, I couldn't get anything. For years I stayed home without a single offer of work of any kind and struggled with pride and shame and deep regret. . .

"One night I was in utter despair. I picked up Mrs. Eddy's book, *Miscellaneous Writings*, and it fell open to the statement (p. 119), 'The nature of the individual, more stubborn than the circumstance, will always be found arguing for itself, — its habits, tastes, and indulgences.'

"I would never read that before, because every time I read it I got resentful saying 'I can't help my nature, I was born this way.' This time I made myself read it and say, 'Every single solitary one of your troubles is the result of the "nature of the individual," not of the outside circumstances or the people you feel have been so unkind to you and all the things you feel have happened to you.' I began to see that what I had wanted was wrong and that I hadn't been willing to be upright, orderly, humble, good, and obedient; and then I was on a better track. The basic uncovering was the fact that I could say, 'Yes, "the nature" — my wants and desires and my false ambitions and my pride — caused all this and would have to go.' It was at last a matter of being willing to admit that to myself. I think that's probably the hardest thing that one has to do. When I finally said, 'Yes, you're right and I will be obedient,' many wonderful things happened.

"I received an offer for a job. There were lots of struggles that first year because it seemed to me that many snarls had to be unwound. Every day I would spend noon hours in Reading Rooms in Beverly Hills. And I worked to be loving, something I'd never done before. All those years when I was so filled with resentment at seeing others ahead of me or more important or better, I was always tired. Gradually, I saw that each person is complete, a complete unit of reflection of the divine. I began to turn away from a sense of competition, to look to my true self and say, 'Thank thee, Father, for I have all that I need.' I tried to look to Mind, Soul, and for the sense of beauty I was created to reflect. I learned just to express the joy that I see and the joy that I feel and the beauty that comes to me.

"I have worked with that same studio, off and on, for all the intervening years. . . The ambition 'to get' has been replaced with the wish 'to give.'"

* * * * *

From *The Christian Science Journal* of September, 1945:

"One young student of Christian Science withdrew from college at the beginning of her junior year and took a position in an advertising agency. In talking with a friend about her new undertaking, she wryly described herself as a 'glorified office boy.' The position was lowly and afforded little remuneration compared with the prestige and ample salaries of her associates, but it provided one outstanding opportunity. The nature of the work was such that she was able to observe copy writers, layout men, and artists at work and could learn much about the relationship of the newspaper to the advertiser, all of which added to the knowledge she would need when she too might be on the production end of the advertising profession...

"Tangible reward for this effort came one happy day when she obtained a new position on the advertising staff of a large retail firm. In securing the place, she laid no claim to wide experience; but her genuine interest in the work and the enthusiastic recommendation of her former employer had been sufficient to bring about a decision in her favor. It was to be a modest beginning, but her expectations were high. She looked forward to happy days of pleasant, interesting work. Prospects for advancement and salary increase looked like certainties of the near future. Her world was, indeed, rosy!

"Reporting to the advertising manager, a very busy and preoccupied individual, she was hurriedly instructed to lay out and write copy for a half-page newspaper advertisement to be finished for an early deadline. Sketchy information on the merchandise was provided; one or two 'do's' and 'don'ts' of the firms's promotion policy were outlined and, with that, the employer was off to a conference. Apparently he had forgotten that allowance was to have been made for the girl's inexperience; that she was to have been given time to learn the work gradually. Dismayed, she thought, 'I can't possibly do it. I need more experience. I'll have to tell him I am not so capable as he thinks.'

"For a moment or two she sat there bewildered and disappointed, offering little resistance to mortal mind's dark prophecies. But there had been other times when she had been tempted to desert her own cause and go over to error's side, when it seemed so much easier to argue for failure instead of success. At such times, when she had really drawn on her knowledge of Christian Science, the angels of God's presence — intelligent, constructive thoughts straight from divine Mind — had so invigorated her consciousness that she had risen to the challenge and had successfully silenced negative arguments. Remembering this now, she realized that these angels were still present, ready to help her to lift her thought above confusion, fear, and a sense of inadequacy.

"She stopped running around in mental circles, and began instead, to declare her oneness with divine Love. As always, Love was ready and waiting to strengthen. Mental poise was re-established when she began to reason something like this: It is true that I have not a wide experience, but 'hitherto hath the Lord helped (me).' (Sam 7:12) It is not the nature of God to lead me up to this point and then desert me. I will continue to trust in Him. I will not be frightened, nor will I accept mortal mind's estimate of my capabilities, but will acknowledge as my own the reflected qualities of intelligence, discrimination, and originality which Mind has bestowed on man.

"As the girl's thinking was calmed by this scientific reasoning, she thought of a familiar statement of Mrs. Eddy's found in *Miscellany*, 'Remember, thou canst be brought into no condition, be it ever so severe, where Love has not been before thee and where its tender lesson is not awaiting thee. Therefore, despair not nor murmur, for that which seeketh to save, to heal, and to deliver, will guide thee, if thou seekest this guidance." Courage and righteous determination began to govern her thinking.

"As a Christian Scientist she well knew that brain or human intellect was no staff upon which to lean. Also she knew that as the expression of God's being, she possessed Godlike qualities and had a right to see them clearly evidenced in this specific circumstance. Love could and would meet the human need. Self-imposed restrictions began to fall away. Now was the time to begin manifesting a larger measure of infinite Mind. She picked up a pencil. Ideas for an arresting, pleasing layout began to take shape on the dummy sheet which lay before her on the desk. Soon she was at her typewriter turning out accurate, inviting copy. Her experience in the advertising agency, working with proof sheets and in daily contact with composing rooms, made it possible now

"I SHALL NOT WANT"

for her to write clear instructions for the printer. Indeed, Love had been with her when she had taken that job, for through it she had become familiar with the mechanics of this work. Within the specified time an acceptable advertisement was ready to be set up.

"Christian Science had again come to her aid not only to meet a need of immediate urgency but also to launch her securely upon the work of her choosing."

* * * * *

From the *Christian Science Sentinel* of January 20, 1945:

"Some years ago, a thoroughly lonesome young man stood at the crossroads of indecision and discouragement. He felt keenly the lack of many good things which are usually considered essential to happiness — satisfying friendships, worthwhile employment, sufficient income — and overshadowing it all was a deep sense of frustration because he had not been able to continue in the profession he had so long prepared for. Again and again there crowded upon his thought the insistent refrain, 'How unhappy I am!' Often the dark fingers of despondency seemed reaching toward him. Being a student of Christian Science, however, he made at least some effort to ward off the evil suggestions which threatened to overwhelm him.

"And then in the midst of all this struggle there suddenly flashed across his thought the startling question, 'Is God unhappy?' A moment of prayerful consideration brought the emphatic answer, 'Certainly not,' for he knew that Christian Science reveals the nature of God as divine Mind, the sum of all true intelligence and goodness. And this Mind must, perforce, be satisfied with its own all-inclusive harmony. He knew, too, that Christian Science reveals man as the expression, or idea, of this Mind, reflecting all the glorious qualities of his creator. Thus, the young man came to the definite conclusion that happiness is a quality of Mind, God, which he could reflect independently of any human surroundings or circumstances. Moreover, he saw that discouragement and downheartedness have nothing to do with this all-present divine Mind; they are but suggestions of a false, carnal mentality.

"All of this spiritual light came as sort of revelation which immediately quieted the sorrow within him. He realized that at that very moment he was free to reflect the unlimited happiness of Mind, God. And Jesus' great promise came to him: 'Seek ye first the kingdom of God (the reign of harmony), . . . and all these things shall be added to you.' It was as though the voice of Truth said to him, 'Seek to express the divine happiness, and all the normal manifestations of goodness will be yours.'

"Thus he saw that joy is the normal result of a conviction that good is real and ever-present; that unless we evidence joy, deep-seated and genuine, we manifestly are not beholding the glorious things which the loving Father has prepared for His children. The goodness of God is so abundantly at hand that he whose eyes are open cannot help imaging forth his gratitude in countenance, in word, and in deed. As he persisted in reflecting the joy whose spiritual source had been revealed to him, he soon found himself in rich possession of those things for which he had longed — true friendships and a far better position and income. Best of all, he had the deep satisfaction of demonstrating that material things, so called, may be the expression, but not the custodians, of happiness."

* * * * *

From the *Christian Science Sentinel* of September 17, 1955, an article tells of an experience in overcoming lack:

"Once he was in an over-populated city, and he had little knowledge of the language spoken there, only a few dollars, no job, and no business acquaintances. He was able to remain undisturbed because he had learned in Christian Science that God provides unlimited good for His children. He held to the true concept of man engaged in his Father's business, instead of the human misconception of a mortal struggling for a personal business in matter.

"Recognizing that man's real employment is to glorify God and bless all His ideas, he endeavored to express more love, humility, patience, joy — the Christly qualities which bear witness to the Father and are needed by all men. He saw that the supply which meets all human needs is actually spiritual. It comes from God, not from a job. It is the inexhaustible flow of spiritual ideas. He had no doubt that his prayer or acknowledgment of spiritual facts, would be answered, for Mrs. Eddy assures us in *Science and Health*, 'Truth is affirmative, and confers harmony.' In one month after his arrival, he was hired by a company for a situation that proved to be interesting and fruitful."

The Spiritual Age

If a few people can demonstrate this law in their individual lives, then gradually increased numbers can use it until it becomes a universal means for overcoming all forms of lack and limitation, and the age-old mesmerism of lack and limitation will be permanently destroyed.

There is another use of this spiritual law that is even more promising in its possibilities. It can become the source of ideas needed to solve the problems that are beyond the natural sciences. It is now obvious that scientific knowledge alone cannot satisfy all of mankind's needs — physical, mental, moral and spiritual. Therefore, we must go beyond the physical sciences into this spiritual realm that scientific methods cannot explore. This realm requires an advanced form of intelligence, a transcending knowledge of spiritual things, in order for us to understand and use its full potential.

Supply

This work requires thinking in a dimension of science and religion that transcends our present concept of them. *Science and Health* lays the foundation for this work, and as we explore Mrs. Eddy's revelation, we find it brings an outpouring of new knowledge. This dimension contains ideas we have not yet conceived of — ideas that can bring about a further evolution of civilization. When these ideas unfold, they are breakthroughs into advanced forms of intelligence that will eventually change, indeed spiritualize, the thinking of the world.

Such unfoldment takes place in vision, creativity, invention. The appearance of this advanced intelligence is inevitable for Mind is always imparting new ideas — ideas that were wholly unknown until the time of their unfoldment to some receptive mind. There is no limit to our capacity for this advanced intelligence except the limit we place on ourselves.

The power of these ideas to bless humanity cannot be measured. Three hundred years ago, the scientific age was nonexistent. Men argued over the strength of God to lift a rock. What made our modern world? Ideas! The steam engine, the cotton gin, the electric light, the Declaration of Independence, the theory of relativity, all began as ideas. Where do these ideas come from? Until now men had supposed that the human mind originated them. But as the spiritual dimension is better understood, and the true source of these ideas is recognized to be the one Mind, we will draw more freely upon this infinite resource outside of and beyond the human mind. Truly, this eternal Mind is already conscious of the answer to every need we have. Through prayer, we can reflect the ideas that solve the problems facing us today.

Seeking right ideas to resolve universal needs is the ultimate use of prayer, for in prayer we work out from unselfed love and a faith that the answers to these problems can be known to us. As we reach out for these ideas, they must appear to us and meet our present need. The scientific age has been a stepping stone

"I shall not want"

to the spiritual age. We must now demonstrate the ideas that bring to the world this further enlightenment. All the means are present to do so. Because Christian Science opens the way to the spiritual realm with its supply of infinite ideas, we can expect a new age, work for it and realize it.

As with the coming of the scientific age, once again the evolution of thought will change man's basic viewpoint and so spiritualize it that humanity will eventually understand how Christ Jesus multiplied the loaves and fishes.

Christ Jesus' unfoldment of an idea and the manifestation of it outwardly were simultaneous. Our present demonstrations of this phenomenon are but man's earliest efforts to emulate the Master's great work. But as we study Christian Science, we will come to understand the spiritual law of supply so thoroughly that we too can feed the multitudes as he did — instantaneously through spiritual means alone.

For further information regarding Christian Science:
Write   The Bookmark
Post Office Box 801143
Santa Clarita, CA 91380
Call   1-800-220-7767
Visit our website: www.thebookmark.com